Peter Jarvis

Universities and Corporate Universities

The Higher Learning Industry in Global Society

KOGAN
PAGE

First published in 2001

Kogan Page Limited
120 Pentonville Road
London N1 9JN
UK

Stylus Publishing Inc.
22883 Quicksilver Drive
Sterling VA 20166-2012
USA

British Library Cataloguing in Publication Data

A CIP record for this book is available from the British Library.

ISBN 0 7494 3404 X (paperback)
     0 7494 3403 1 (hardback)

Typeset by JS Typesetting, Wellingborough, Northants
Printed and bound by Creative Print and Design (Wales) Ebbw Vale

Contents

Preface   vii

About the author   ix

1. Universities under pressure   1
The changing status of the university 3; Changing student
clientele 6; The universities and the marketplace for learning 8;
The changing forms of knowledge 11; The changing nature of
research 14; Changing methods of delivery of programmes 15;
The changing role of the academic 17; Conclusion 18

2. Globalization and its implications   20
The processes of economic globalization 20; The nation
state and universities 29; The university and its region 32;
Conclusion 35

3. Knowledge and the knowledge society   37
The nature of the knowledge society 38; The nature of
knowledge 40; Practical knowledge 46; Research 50;
Managing knowledge 53; Conclusion 56

4. From teaching to learning   58
The dissemination of knowledge 58; Teaching 60; From
teaching to learning 61; Lifelong learning 65; Innovations in
teaching 69; Distance education 72; Learning and research
74; Conclusion 76

5. Universities and the learning society   77
The learning society 77; Learning cities 88; The learning
organization 91; Conclusion 94

6. **The corporate university (academy) of the university**   **96**
    The corporate nature of the university 97; The university's
    corporate academy (university) 103; Universities at the
    crossroads 107; Conclusion 109

7. **The corporate university**   **111**
    The history and expansion of the corporate university 112;
    Characteristics and programmes of corporate universities 116;
    Corporate universities as universities 122; Conclusion 128

8. **The lifelong learning industry**   **129**
    The corporate universities 132; The universities 135;
    Conclusion 138

9. **What is the university?**   **140**
    The concept of 'university' 142; The distinctive features of
    traditional universities 145; Discourse about the university 147;
    Conclusion 149

References   *150*

Index   *162*

Preface

This is certainly an age of learning when more people are seeking education at every level, but paradoxically it is one in which higher education – especially the university sector – appears to be in crisis. There are many reasons for this including: the expansion of the sector from one which has catered for the elite to one providing higher education to a wider section of the population; chronic underfunding from government and the need to become more self-financing; the growth in demand for continuing professional education from all the knowledge-based occupations.

These increasing pressures have also caused scholars of higher education to stop and ask the question – what is the university? This is a pertinent question since the polytechnics in the UK, for example, were granted university status a decade ago and around the world we see people's universities, universities of the third age and now corporate universities. Are these latter forms 'real' universities? What is a 'real' university?

This book offers a sociological analysis of what has occurred in the university sector of higher education since globalization took off in the 1970s. It examines the nature of globalization and suggests that its forces underlie both the emergence of the knowledge society and, consequently, the learning society. Both concepts are discussed and related to university education. However, the emergence of the corporate universities is the other main focus of this book – do they represent a failure in some way of higher education or even of further education to respond to the pressures generated by contemporary society?

The churches and then the states and civic authorities founded the universities, and now it is the corporations. But what type of universities are they founding? The nature of the corporate universities is examined within the context of lifelong learning and questions asked about how they relate to the traditional universities – partners or competitors, both or neither?

Finally, we return to the question of the nature of the university and it is suggested that universities are a part of the institutionalized sector of humankind's quest for truth, a truth that is ultimately unknowable. But the quest provides some answers to the questions, even if they are of a temporary nature, and the learning process is one through which people grow and develop.

I have worked in universities full-time for almost 25 years, as an educator of adults. Frequently, I have been frustrated by the slowness with which they move and their inability to adapt to the demands that adults of all ages have made upon them. I have also been employed, on a part-time basis, by the British Open University since it began. I still teach for it after all these years as I have been committed to lifelong education ever since I became an adult educator. Constantly I have been amazed by the inability of universities to learn the lessons that their extramural departments have learnt over the years and yet I appreciate the cautiousness with which they have thought that they have had to move into new territory.

This book, then, represents the attempts of an educator of adults to understand the changes that are occurring – it also reflects my sympathy both with the need for rapid social change and with the need for universities to retain their own identity in the face of tremendous social pressures.

The book has been written for all who work in higher education, but also for those who work in further education and in education and training. It has also been written for scholars in the field of lifelong education and for those who make policy and offer strategies for development. It is hoped that it will throw some more light on the processes that are occurring in universities and help policy makers understand a little more the social context within which they operate.

About the author

Peter Jarvis is Professor of Continuing Education in the School of Educational Studies at the University of Surrey, where he is also convenor of the Centre for Research in Lifelong Learning. He is also adjunct professor of adult education at the University of Georgia, in the USA. In addition, he teaches sociology, part-time, for the Open University. He holds degrees from the universities of London, Sheffield, Birmingham, Aston and Surrey and has been awarded honorary doctorates from the University of Helsinki and Fairfax University. He is also a Fellow of the Royal Society of Arts. In 1990, he was awarded a scholarship by the Japan Society for the promotion of Science at the University of Tokyo.

His work, having sociological and philosophical foundations, has focused mainly on learning, the education of adults and lifelong learning. He has taught teacher, vocational, and continuing education and has undertaken research in adult learning and a number of other projects. He has also been involved in distance education for many years.

In 1988, he was awarded the Cyril O Houle World Award for Literature in Adult Education by the American Association of Adult and Continuing Education. He was also awarded the Comenius Award of the European Society for Voluntary Associations in 1997 and, in the same year, conducted into the International Hall of Fame for Adult Educators in America.

He is the author of many books; among his latest are *Adult and Continuing Education: Theory and Practice* (second edition, Routledge, 1995), *Ethics and the Education of Adults in Late Modern Society* (NIACE, 1997), *International Dictionary of Adult and Continuing Education* (Kogan Page, 1999), *The Practitioner Researcher: Developing Theory from Practice* (Jossey Bass, 1999) and *Learning in Later Life* (Kogan Page, 2001). He has also recently written *The Human Resource Development Handbook* with Pat Hargreaves (revised edition, Kogan Page, 2000) and *Theory and Practice of Learning* with John Holford and Colin Griffin (Kogan Page, 1998). In addition, he has edited a number of books, the latest being

The Age of Learning (Kogan Page, 2001). He has also written many papers and chapters in books and his work has been widely translated.

Peter Jarvis is the founding editor of *The International Journal of Lifelong Education* and serves on the editorial boards of a number of journals. He is a frequent speaker and lecturer on adult, continuing and higher education, and lifelong learning, in many parts of the world.

1

Universities under pressure

Most of the early universities were founded, in Europe, by the Church. After the Enlightenment they were established by the state and civic governments and now, in the time of late modernity, new universities are being founded by the corporations. Higher education is certainly changing; indeed the changes are prompting the question – what is the university? But that is no new question for implicitly the changes in the university system after the Enlightenment also posed the same question. Perhaps there is no blueprint of the university because, like education in general, it has always adjusted in response to the demands of society's dominant institutions, whether they are Church, state or transnational corporations. This is one of the questions that we will keep on confronting throughout this book.

Barnett (1990) might not totally concur, as he has endeavoured to delineate a number of characteristics of higher education, although he acknowledges (2000) that universities no longer know precisely what they are. He recognized that universities have been exposed to a considerable crisis and that we do not have a set of foundation principles by which we can delineate higher education:

> It is a crisis to do with the way that we understand higher education, the fundamental principles on which the idea of higher education has traditionally stood, and the way in which these principles are undermined (Barnett, 1990, p 3).

But the pressure on the universities is not just because we do not understand the principles, it is also certain that the changes in the contemporary knowledge-based society are causing strain in the more traditional institutions of higher education in the Western world. This has produced a flood of literature on the subject (Katz *et al*, 1999; Levine *et al*, 1990; Lucas, 1996;

Pelikan, 1992; Scott, 1984; Seville and Tooley, 1997; Shumar, 1997; Sinnott and Johnson, 1996, *inter alia*). In addition, the pressures are working through to the academic staff. Kinman (2000, p 18) for instance, records how 70 per cent found their jobs stressful, 53 per cent complained of poor physiological health and 25 per cent had taken time off work because of stress-related illness. Yet, paradoxically, they still retained a high degree of job satisfaction. Indeed, Goddard, A (2000a, p 1) reported that academics work an average of 55 hours a week with some working as many as 70 hours for no additional financial reward. This situation is one which governments and employers can, and do, exploit to their own ends and to the cost of the academics suffering the stress (Shumar, 1997). This is, incidentally, similar to the situation found in health and welfare services at the present time.

Since the 1970s, the universities have been more exposed to the substructural pressures of society to change. In the UK, for example, this process was exacerbated at the beginning of the 1980s by the right-wing monetarist government that abolished academic tenure and decreased the funding levels of the universities, forcing them to become more market oriented and competitive. This has resulted in many of the traditional universities assuming a more corporate form and functioning more like the corporations; indeed many a University Court meeting is rather like a company annual general meeting with a financial profit and loss report taking a prominent place on the agenda. The vice-chancellors have also become chief executive officers; collegial governance is disappearing, and so on (Brandon, 1999). Indeed, the abolition of tenure for academics in the UK signalled a major status change in the position of university academics – they are no longer holders of a property but employees and workers. Universities have become like corporations and are being forced to rethink their mission, or their function, in this changing society.

This chapter will explore some of the changes that are occurring in the higher education system, illustrate how the wider social pressures are being exerted on it and on academic staff and note how the system is reacting to them. Let it also be said from the outset that change creates space that enables innovation and experimentation, and for those universities that are able to respond, there are exciting and challenging times ahead – whether the outcome will be a recognizable university is another matter. Those who have a vision and the will may grow and develop, but those universities bogged down by internal politics, bureaucratic procedures and traditionalism may well suffer the long-term consequences and lose influence, a significant role in future higher education opportunities, and even their own independent existence. Indeed, change can create problems and stresses that inhibit the take-up of the opportunities that this new space has created.

This chapter will outline seven major areas of change that have occurred in recent years as a result of these wider pressures. Naturally there is considerable overlap between these areas but in the following discussion this will be restricted to a minimum:

- the changing status of the university;
- changing student clientele;
- the universities and the marketplace for learning;
- the changing forms of knowledge;
- the changing nature of research;
- changing methods of delivery of programmes;
- the changing role of the academic.

In this initial discussion no attempt will be made to prioritize any of the above. We will return to all of these points again at various places in this book. The fundamental argument of the whole study is that higher education is caught up in the forces of globalization that are creating pressures for change in every walk of life. Nevertheless, if the universities respond chameleon-like to these pressures, society will lose one of its potential bastions for democracy and institutions that exist for the wider good of humanity. In addition, if they did so, there could be a major loss in the study of the arts and humanities, and other minority disciplines.

But from the outset it will be shown that the universities cannot be totally isolated from the wider global and social pressures although some governments, such as the Finnish (Ministry of Education, 1999) have shielded their university system from some of these social pressures far more than have those of the UK or the USA. Consequently, national governments can and, as many academics would argue, should be more involved in protecting rather than regulating higher education in a world knowledge economy.

The changing status of the university

From their earliest times, the most powerful institutions in society have established universities for their own ends. The churches in Europe were among the earliest institutions to do so. Here the priests were trained, theology and the Bible studied, and law and medicine expounded, for these were also part of the revealed knowledge controlled by the Church in the name of the God who was regarded as the creator, sustainer and saviour of the world. Those who occupied the prestigious professorial chairs in the universities were frequently rich and powerful clerics; they controlled and legitimated the knowledge that underlay the whole social structure, knowledge that offered the way of eternal salvation for the people. Naturally, there were changes as a result of the Reformation, which was a secularizing force in itself, leading to the industrialization of Britain, but the traditional world view was still controlled by the churches.

With the Enlightenment and the outset of the modernity era, Western culture was gradually changed. None of the major *philosophes* who led the Enlightenment thinking occupied one of those prestigious university professorial appointments, although Adam Smith was one who had held such a position previously. Free from the intellectually crippling power of the Church and from the universities, they were able to think afresh on the fundamental questions of cosmology and humanity. Subsequently, the intellectual power of the Church was undermined and a new social order was inaugurated which emphasized, among other things, reason and rationality, empiricism, science, universalism, progress, individualism, toleration, freedom, uniformity of human nature and secularism (Hamilton, 1992, pp 21–22). Not all of these values were new with the Enlightenment since rationality, individualism and a scientific orientation to the world, among others, were embedded within Reformation Protestantism, especially Calvinism (see Merton, 1968, pp 628–81). Entrepreneurial capitalism also emerged in this period with its close relationship to Calvinism (Weber, 1971), as did the modern state (Held, 1992), and these were to affect the development of the modern university.

With the Industrial Revolution and the Enlightenment, a new emphasis on empirical science and the political processes emerged. Knowledge in the form of the academic disciplines that have been a common feature of modernity, was taught in new universities established by state and civil authorities. Empirical scientific knowledge, which replaced the revealed knowledge of theology, became the basis of the dominant subjects studied and scientific research became quite central to them. Knowledge was their business. In the West, the capitalist system became the central force of society although it was still regarded as part of civil society, but as the years of the modernity project passed there were increasing claims that the state was being controlled by capitalism. Even so, for many the state was still regarded as the central governing mechanism and, within a pluralistic governmental structure, the universities developed a form of independence, allowing them to continue to play a major role in society. However, with the development of the major professions there were also other authoritative advisers to governments. The universities, which had helped to educate the professionals, took their place with the professions in advising governments. The possession of knowledge, however, was still a means of accessing power and the universities were the institutions that helped prepare young men to hold these powerful and influential positions in society – the university's focus was on those individuals who were to become the elite!

At the same time, as education became one of the means by which the state managed society, higher education retained its high status, since it provided entry to those individuals who were to constitute both the elite who governed and the upper classes who worked with and advised them. They even legislated for what was the correct knowledge. But society was becoming more pluralistic and more authorities emerged making the intellectual voice in the affairs of state only one among a number, so the universities assumed the role of interpreting the various schools of thought in society. As Bauman (1987, p 145) points out, intellectuals could still perform the role of legislating knowledge within their own academic discipline but beyond it they had become interpreters of different cultural traditions. In a major sense, this was the period when intellectuals were losing their political power, or as Bauman (1992, p 16) so nicely expressed it:

> The House of Solomon is now placed in a prosperous suburb, far away from ministerial buildings and military headquarters, where it can enjoy in peace, undisturbed, the elegant life of mind complete with not inconsiderable material comfort. Intellectual freedom is not something to be treated lightly. It offers a unique chance to make the matters of intellectual concern into a total, self-contained and self-sufficient form of life; and it offers the practitioners of such a form of life the gratifying feeling of being in full and exclusive control of the life process and its products. . . Given the memory of the intimate link between political engagement and intellectual unfreedom, the autonomy of intellectual discourse turns into a highly attractive value in its own right.

But even this was to change. Throughout this period both capitalism and its industrial technological base were growing in strength. New commodities needing greater technological knowledge to produce were requiring more highly trained people to create and design them. Gradually pressures were being placed on universities to update those individuals working in these fields, but universities found these pressures difficult to respond to, especially when it was not only updating that was required but also producing greater numbers of recruits for the knowledge-based industries. The role of the universities was changing from serving the state in managing society to serving industry and commerce in ensuring people are employable. Employability has become a symbol of societal membership, almost akin to citizenship, and the universities provide a route into full membership.

Through the period which seems to be bringing the era of modernity to a close, the voice of industry and commerce has been increasingly critical of the university system, and as its demands grew so the business world assumed a greater role in education and training of its own workers and eventually the corporate universities were born (Eurich, 1985; Meister, 1998), including the University for Industry in the UK. Traditional universities are endeavouring to enter partnerships with industry and commerce to gain more students and to train their workforces, which does offer exciting opportunities, but if they do not succeed then industry and commerce can afford to operate their own educational system independently. Now the universities prepare people for the world of work and maintain them in it, rather than preparing the society's governing elite and its advisers. The state now ensures that the universities do this job efficiently through quality inspections and so forth. In other words, the state now regulates the process of preparing the workforce and ensures that individuals are and remain employable members of the emerging global society that exists in part, paradoxically, because of deregulation.

Changing student clientele

As Western society is becoming a knowledge-based society, so industry and commerce are demanding a higher level of education from their new recruits, and demanding a greater number of recruits who have that level of education. Traditionally universities have accepted a relatively small percentage of school leavers and trained them for the elite positions in society, and many of those who have undertaken postgraduate study and research have been destined for the knowledge elite of the university academic staff. But with the advent of the knowledge society, this has changed. In 1991, it was estimated that knowledge workers constituted some 20 per cent of the workforce in the USA, whereas in the 1950s it was no more than 8 per cent (Reich, 1991, p 179). Reich (1991, p 229) argued that knowledge workers need to be educated in abstract thinking, system thinking, experimentation and collaboration – which are the types of skill basic to a university education. But that means that at least 20 per cent of school leavers – even more since the service professions also demand similar skills – need to have those educational opportunities. Increasingly the knowledge society demands a greater number of knowledge-based recruits to its workforce. Consequently, universities have had to face the introduction of mass higher education in recent years, something totally unfamiliar to the traditional university ethos. But they have not received a great deal of additional funding to cope with the growing demands and, as a result, the workload of academic staff has increased considerably.

However, it is not merely an increasing number of undergraduates that are required. As new knowledge is generated, so the universities are being asked to provide continuing education for the knowledge workers – more taught masters courses, and even practitioner doctoral courses are being introduced. People who might never have attended university or those who only came once during their lifetime are now enrolling two or three times for award-bearing courses. There is a gradual recognition that since the knowledge that these learners require is pragmatic and integrated, and that much postgraduate education should relate specifically to work, courses need to be more project-based, or indeed located in the workplace itself. This requires a new conceptualization of postgraduate courses, new approaches to teaching and learning and a great deal of time to develop relevant programmes. In addition, assessment is becoming much more about the successful completion of a project that works in practice rather than about 'correct knowledge', although learners are being required to show an awareness of why it works, or otherwise. The knowledge is practical and since it is work-based and integrated it tends to be multidisciplinary rather than orientated to a single discipline. Universities are being forced to recon-ceptualize and restructure their assessment system and they are also beginning to place more emphasis upon quality at the point of delivery than ever before.

However, this expansion of higher education into lifelong learning is not just a trend for taught courses, it is also a trend in research. Increasingly people researching for PhDs are part-time; their research is work-based with their fees often being paid by their employers. Additionally, the idea that the doctorate was a route into university employment has changed. Full-time postgraduate study is becoming a minority form of postgraduate work.

Indeed, part-time study at every level is becoming a major form of higher education, and even as early as 1986/7, 39 per cent of all home students in higher education in the UK were part time (Tight, 1991, p 22). Traditional universities are not equipped to cope with part-time students working unsocial hours. University administrators are used to running bureaucratic organizations catering for full-time residential students, for whom the procedures have been designed.

At the same time as universities are being asked to respond to the dominant demands of industry and commerce, they are also being expected to play a social role. Having formerly catered for the elite, they are now also being asked to reach out and recruit students from minority and socially excluded groups. Widening participation has become another aspect of the universities' mission to provide opportunity to individuals who have not been able to benefit from the school system, or who have been failed by it. Naturally, it is right that the elite emphasis should be replaced by this more egalitarian system, but this new demand also adds to the workload of academic staff and to the complexity of the university – both as a concept and as an institution (Preece, 1999).

Normal routes have been altered and other forms of entry to the university have been introduced in order to widen participation. Accreditation of Prior Learning and Accreditation of Prior Experiential Learning are gradually becoming accepted in some universities as entry routes. Universities and departments have established committees to assess accreditation of prior learning, and so academic staff are now also undertaking a new role, one traditionally performed by the school examining boards, which is eating into the time that can be devoted to academic work. This role is important in helping more people gain places in universities but it is also time consuming. However, such assessments are also subjective (as most assessments are) but, in the marketplace of learning, there are instances where the system functions in the same way as the retail market offering discount bargains. Discount selling is a means of undercutting competitors and this is now occurring in the competitive learning market.

The universities and the marketplace for learning

The conditions that have been created in the UK are such that universities are underfunded by government – a strategy that ensures that they earn income by responding to the demands from potential fee-paying students or their employers. This forces them to be much more flexible and also ensures that fees are competitive. At the same time it undermines any independence that the universities had to play a democratic role in society. Universities are now in a marketplace seeking students; they have directors of marketing and courses are prepared not because the academic disciple demands it but because there is a market for them. Universities are even teaching the 'academic discipline' of entrepreneurship, but of course it is not an academic discipline in the traditional sense because, as we shall note below, many more courses are becoming practically orientated.

Education has become a commodity to be sold in the marketplace of learning (Shumar, 1997); this process has been intensified because of the advances made in distance education. In the UK, there is now 'e-education' and soon, if ministers get their way, the 'e-university' – and in some countries of the world, such as Singapore, most new courses are prepared for online delivery. Of course this is also happening elsewhere in the first world, including the USA, and the UK is merely part of the same social process. However, education costs money and in the UK government has restricted grants to universities and to students because of, among other things, the enormous growth in higher education. Universities are now recipients of large grants from corporations, all of which orientate them to respond to priorities from the corporate donor agencies – and education is becoming a service industry. Many undergraduates have to borrow money for their higher education, and even work part time in order to complete their studies. While some post-graduate students gain funding from their employers, others have to finance themselves. Higher educational institutions are money earners in the learning market. While the market generates flexibility, it is also foreign to welfare and academia; it still favours those who can afford to purchase its commodities and the price may become more important than the quality to the purchasers. Despite all the work of agencies like the UK's Quality Assurance Agency, flexibility rather than quality was discovered to be the main reason why corporations would cooperate with universities in the USA (Meister, 1998, p 184). Being an Ivy League college was the least important factor for industry when seeking partnerships with the universities.

Fundamentally, it is not education that is the commodity, it is knowledge since this has become a knowledge society (Stehr, 1994). In the marketplace of knowledge, there has to be some indication that the knowledge has been obtained and consumed, so that there is a need for some form of accreditation from a university, or as Baudrillard (1988, p 22) suggests, 'consumption, in so far as it is meaningful, is a *systematic act of the manipulation of signs*'. (Emphasis in the original.) The significance of knowledge is well illustrated by Lyotard (1984, p 5):

> Knowledge in the form of an informational commodity indispensable to productive power is already, and will continue to be, a major – perhaps *the* major – stake in the world-wide competition for power. It is conceivable that the nation-states will one day fight for the control of information, just as they battled in the past for the control of territory, and afterwards for the control of access to and exploitation of raw materials and cheap labor. (Emphasis in the original.)

Indeed, industrial espionage is already well known and competition in the knowledge society is intense. New commodities have to be brought to market, products have to be manufactured at the lowest cost, and so on. In labour-intensive industries the main way to keep the costs low is to pay the producers of the commodities as low a salary as possible. This we see happening in many industries, where only those in top management are paid high salaries while their employees receive far lower rates of pay. University teachers have now been reclassified as workers and this same process of cost-cutting is being applied to them. More significantly, it is cheaper to employ part-time staff to teach courses that others have prepared, in a similar manner to the Open University employing part-time associate lecturers, than it is to retain a full complement of full-time staff. The old maxim 'overworked and underpaid' is frequently heard around universities, but the issue of overwork can also mean that quality falls and, consequently, government and the employers have introduced quality assurance procedures in order to try to retain the academic standards. These procedures are, to a very great extent, a bureaucratic mechanism that seeks to review all the documentation and allow the claim that the standards in the majority of institutions are acceptable, but a few institutions might have to be brought into line from time to time. Universities work hard to produce the necessary documentation – which adds more both to the workload and to the stress of staff. It is hard to see, indeed doubtful, that the actual quality itself has improved, but there is a great deal of rhetoric that surrounds the process. It might reasonably be claimed that the validation procedures that universities themselves have introduced have meant that academics do think through the implications of their innovations a little more rigorously than they might have done in the past. Paradoxically, these very procedures that have been put in place to ensure quality also make the universities more like bureaucratic organizations with a top-heavy management structure making more demands on the worker-academics, and making universities less flexible and more cumbersome in a marketplace that demands rapid response to its demands. Indeed, Eurich (1985, p 15), commenting on American higher education, wrote:

> Differences in mission between the two systems have led, however, to marked contrast in styles that hamper cooperation. Higher education enjoys a more leisurely and wider time frame with such traditional academic routines as 50-minute class hours three times a week. Some say the routines are hardened, rigid, and encrusted to their own detriment. To the corporate world, with its pattern of short-term, intensive hours, and highly motivated employee-students, academia appears luxurious. In their world 'time frames' are costly and company controls well understood.

These are lessons that academics are learning, but the nature of academia is different from the commercial world. It does take time to produce scholarship and good teaching materials, and these are suffering in the present marketplace of learning despite the quality assurance mechanisms and to the chagrin of many of the academic staff who often feel that they do not have the time or support to maintain the highest standards. Both time and support staff are costly entities in the marketplace!

However, it has to be recognized that many of the universities have endeavoured to retain and research subjects that are not marketable in the traditional sense. Studies in academic areas that relate to our history and our culture, to the citizenship and welfare of the people and to humanity itself are still part of the university mission. These are not necessarily marketable in quite the same manner as are the areas demanded by business and commerce, so they need the support of a government that is clearly failing to invest sufficient funds into the university system for it to maintain, let alone improve on, its present standards across the spectrum of academic subjects taught and researched in the university.

The changing forms of knowledge

Those early Western universities were concerned mostly with revealed, or received, knowledge. Scholars endeavoured to understand the teaching and implications of the Christian Church and the Bible and to disseminate them to their students, and they also endeavoured to understand the classical texts of the ancient Greek and Roman worlds. The universities were at best institutions of teaching and scholarship. With the secularizing forces of the Industrial Revolution and the Enlightenment much of this was to be challenged.

Emphasis was placed upon empirical knowledge discovered through scientific method, and rational thought became the basis of the philosophical tradition. Gradually the accepted foundations of knowledge shifted from received to empirical and rational knowledge that was then understood within the emerging framework of the academic disciplines. Empirical research was added to scholarship as the non-teaching functions of the academic increased. New universities emerged during this period which emphasized the values of the Enlightenment, and the old universities gradually incorporated these new perspectives within their curricula.

At the same time as this was happening in Europe, another approach to knowledge was gaining ground in the USA. Philosophers such as James ([1907] 1995) turned away from looking at the foundations and began to look at the consequences:

> No particular results then, so far, but only an attitude of orientation, is what the pragmatic method means. *The attitude of looking away from first things, principles, 'categories' supposed necessities; and of looking towards last things, fruits, consequences, facts.* (p 22, emphasis in the original)

This approach to knowledge was embedded in the new universities being established in the USA in the second half of the 19th century. These were the Land-Grant Colleges, established as a result of the Morrill Act in 1861, which incorporated the idea of useful knowledge (see Kett, 1994, p 127). While familiar to educators in Western Europe, it was not incorporated very easily into the high-status university curricula. However, pragmatism has gained in importance in recent years, and Lyotard (1984) has argued that performativity reflects the pragmatics of science and, he might have added, of capitalism. This practical orientation has greatly influenced university curricula in recent years leading to more vocationally and practically orientated education, to the process of modularization and an integrated approach to knowledge. This type of knowledge has been discussed in Gibbons *et al* (1994) as Mode 2 knowledge production, wrongly giving the impression that it is a new approach to knowledge; Aristotle (1925, pp 137–58) discussed this in great detail. Even so, it is probably the main form of knowledge production that underlies the corporate classroom (see also Nyiri and Smith, 1988).

These three conditions of knowledge – philosophical/rational, empirical and pragmatic – underlie epistemological studies (Scheffler, 1965), although three further questions remain in relation to knowledge and the university: the speed of knowledge change, the relationship between knowledge and information, and the nature of reflective thought.

In the 1920s, the German sociologist Max Scheler ([1926] 1980, p 76), recognizing the relativity of different forms of knowledge, attempted to classify knowledge into seven types based upon their speed of change, with the slowest at the top of this list and the fastest at the bottom:

1. myth and legend;
2. knowledge implicit in everyday natural language;
3. religious knowledge;
4. mystical knowledge;
5. philosophic-metaphysical knowledge;
6. positive knowledge;
7. technological knowledge.

This typology will be examined more thoroughly in Chapter 3. It may be seen that the forms of knowledge underlying the changing university are all included here, but Scheler distinguished between the first five and the last two. The latter he called 'artificial knowledge' since they change 'hour by hour' and do not have time to get embedded in the culture of a society before they are changed. He was keen to locate the reason for the change in human drives, although he did acknowledge other wider forces. More significantly, the forces of the capitalist system drive positive and technological knowledge to change at a much faster pace than when Scheler originally conducted his study. Such speed of change has profound effects on the universities that seek to offer courses of study in the latest developments in knowledge.

The forces of change and developments in adult learning theory have begun to call into question the nature of knowledge itself and the relationship between theory and practice. Basically it has been argued elsewhere (Jarvis, 1999) that each practice situation is unique and ephemeral so that while practitioners bring their own developing experience to each one, they have still to learn something new in every situation they enter. This means that in process terms they are going to work out for themselves pragmatically what is possible for them and to follow those procedures until they no longer work – then they will have to experiment again in the workplace. They were creating their own unique practical knowledge. Fundamentally, they are not applying theory to practice, since any theory they learnt in the university reflected a previous situation – so that the theory with which they are presented is information not knowledge. It is information to be tried out in practice, and recognizes that valid knowledge is learnt in practice and this demands that universities rethink their role and also the way in which they validate learning. (See also Marsick and Watkins, 1990.)

Not all change is necessarily good and universities do not merely exist to respond to the pressures of social change, even though they are being increasingly forced into this position. Habermas (1972) reminded us that apart from the technical and practical approaches to human enquiry there is another that he called an 'emancipatory cognitive interest', which is basically independent thought. The extent to which this can happen is debatable in a system financially dependent upon the powerful institutions of the capitalist world. What is not debatable is that there has always been an independent critical form of knowledge – it might be called ideological within the present framework but it is no more ideological than many other forms of knowledge. Universities have traditionally embraced this position, seeing themselves as bastions of free speech and critical analysis in democratic society. In a variety of different ways this has been undermined in a number of Western societies, including the UK, and academics feel that they are losing some of the freedoms that they have had to undertake their own studies and publicize freely their own conclusions, freedoms that were protected by tenure.

The changing nature of research

Despite all the apparent noise made about research and the Research Assessment Exercise in the UK, the average research effort in the European Union does not compare favourably with that in either the USA or Japan. Moreover, even in the EU, in 1998 the UK spent a smaller proportion of its Gross Domestic Product on research and development than did Denmark, the Netherlands, France, Germany, Finland or Sweden (European Union, 2000). At the same time a great deal of time in universities is spent in applying for these restricted and competitive funds, and the research itself has become focused. Long and tedious application forms have to be prepared taking many days of academic time, which has served to add to the ever-increasing workload of academics. That both they and their departments are then assessed through another long and tedious set of forms on the success of their research is but another indication of the centralization and bureaucratization of the system. Some academics are now refusing to complete such forms, considering that the investment of time and energy in such applications is not justified by the success rate. Lucas (1996, p 191) writes of American academic staff:

> Those committed to teaching find themselves torn between their concern for supplying high-quality instruction in the classroom (always a time-consuming undertaking if done well) and the demands of grant-writing and project management, of research and publication that are viewed as essential for professional advancement within their home institution and within their discipline.

And the USA spends a greater proportion of its Gross Domestic Product on research than does the UK! Significantly, this raises the question about whether some universities need to become teaching universities and others research universities – a question often posed but as yet, one that remains unanswered because of the additional problems it will create. We will suggest another division in the final chapter of this study. Mechanisms, such as the Research Assessment Exercise in the UK, have been designed to reform the system gradually, but few universities wish to be regarded as only teaching universities since research has been seen as a major indicator of the quality, even the essence, of the university since the Enlightenment. Other scholars conclude that there are not really separate fields in any case, since this is a feature of the late modern world (Jarvis, 1999; Katz *et al,* 1999, p 31). But perhaps *the* university is an anachronism today.

Research endeavours are increasingly being undertaken in partnership with, or at the behest of, government and large corporations which both fund the research and then use the results for their own ends. Such partnerships are valid and they can yield considerable satisfaction and great opportunities for researchers. At the same time, they are also indicative of a degree of lost autonomy in academic research, and even of the loss of the 'pure' research potential that universities have always had but have frequently failed to exploit. In the UK, some of the blame, if there is blame to be apportioned, for this must be located in government's unwillingness to increase its research budget to the level of some of the wealthier European countries.

More significantly, professional practitioners are increasingly undertaking research into their own practice (Jarvis, 1999) and they are generating new knowledge. Practice itself has become a base for both learning and research and universities are being forced to adjust to examining such research in the increasing number of taught and research higher degree programmes being offered. Academic supervisors may no longer be the subject experts or the legislators of correct knowledge in the research area in which they are supervising since they may be unfamiliar with the workplace of the part-time research student. However, they have to become expert research methodologists in order to supervise and assess these research projects.

Research is increasingly being conducted away from the universities, in the corporations' own research laboratories and by other private agencies. Corporations are investing vast amounts of capital (financial and intellectual) in research and development – far more than governments. Often the results of this research are not placed in the public domain. This is often true when a university academic has been contracted to undertake research for a private company, so that the nature of academic research itself is changing. The university has lost the monopoly control that it had on research and generating new knowledge. This raises the question about the nature of the university itself – for what reason does it exist?

Changing methods of delivery of programmes

There is a sense in which the creation of the British Open University heralded the start of a new era in university education. It was not the first university to utilize distance education methods but it reflected the spirit of the age (Groombridge, 1972) and it was a catalyst for change (Rumble and Harry, 1982). Many countries followed the Open University's lead and, although traditional academics tended to be a little sceptical in those early years, it is now a mega-university and its course material is widely used.

Traditional academics, used to face-to-face teaching, are now confronted with having to produce learning materials that can be utilized in a variety of delivery techniques and used in a multitude of different countries. For example, at the time of writing, the University of Surrey's MSc in Applied Professional Studies in Education and Training is being taught at a distance in over 30 countries. But before many academics have learnt to write competent distance education materials to be used in the more traditional approaches to distance education, they are being asked to be involved in more sophisticated and hi-tech approaches, and all of this without a great deal of training for these new roles. It is not just preparing lectures, but being involved in video-sessions, e-mail tutorials, video-conferencing, supervising research dissertations at a distance and teaching individuals whom they may never meet in the flesh. More significantly, every presentation of learning materials on the Web is in the public domain and can be accessed and assessed by a wider public that the traditional mode of face-to-face teaching.

The participants also have access to a new form of library on the Internet. Consequently, the whole future of residential education is open to further discussion – perhaps students need spend a lot less time on the campuses and more time on their laptops or personal computers. New forms of residential education become possible and they need not all be full-time. Naturally, it might be argued that the learning experience is different but it can also be argued that it might be cheaper than residential education.

The utilization of electronic methods of delivery means that students can access courses from different universities and this might call for new methods of validation and new approaches to academic cooperation. Why duplicate teaching when two universities are running the same course and both putting it on the Web? Academic staff may have to be shared between different institutions, and so on. Universities are being driven to discover new forms of organization and cooperation – but there are still those who prefer to bury their heads in the sand and hope that these present conditions will go away! Academic staff are already under a great deal of stress, and yet the changes that this will introduce may be even more far-reaching.

Farringdon (1999, p 90), commenting on this potential suggests:

> The fact is that educators already have at their disposal a great variety of new software tools for teaching, and the number will only grow. Using them effectively requires fresh thinking. Truly improving education with the new media will require faculty to start with a blank page, to explore how best to teach each course, and to listen closely to students as they comment on whether it really works.

Taking advantage of the new media to improve education in this fundamental way is not a casual business. Exploiting the power of the World Wide Web in teaching is not necessarily simple or inexpensive. Faculty will need substantial help in terms of staff support and equipment. More importantly, faculty will have to pay far more attention to innovation in teaching than has been common in the past, and administrators will have to reward them for it.

All of this at a time when apparent quality assessment has induced a cautious approach to change in order to avoid criticism and poor assessment reports, and governments are seeking to hold down financial support for higher education!

The changing role of the academic

It has often been noted that education has shifted from the teacher to the learner, and the role of the teacher has been redefined as a facilitator of learning. However, it is now learning *per se* that is at the heart of this new phenomenon in which universities are engaged. Learning materials can be purchased in the market; so who is now the teacher? Is the teacher the person(s) who prepare the learning information, or those who actually prepare the materials, or those who deliver the materials, or those who assess the learning (if this is undertaken)? Is the teacher the educator in the traditional educational institution or the human resource developer in industry and commerce? Is the teacher the mentor who assists the learner, or the counsellor or adviser whose role is to offer support and guidance? Clearly the role of the teacher has changed, but the factors that remain constant are the learner and learning. Consequently, it now becomes possible to begin to identify the variety of role players who might be regarded as teachers of adults.

In traditional education when time and space intersected, the teaching role was much clearer than it is now. The realignment of time and space has resulted in a division of labour in the role of the teacher, which Table 1.1 (see page 18) begins to explore. It must be recognized that these are not all separate roles in every teaching and learning event and they may not always be performed by the same person.

It is no wonder that phrases like 'jobbing academic' and 'generalist' are frequently found within the language of university staff – they may wish to be genuine specialists in their area of knowledge but the demands are so great for them to perform so many roles that they experience great stress. Yet at

Table 1.1 The division of labour in teaching

In contact with the learners	At one stage removed from learners	At two stages removed from learners
Teacher/facilitator	Trainer of teachers/trainers	Researcher
Teaching assistant	Author(s) of learning materials	Writer of research proposals/reports
Trainer	Programme/curriculum planners	Author of academic papers/books
Mentor	Programme administrative staff	
Counsellor/adviser	Programme technical staff	
Education administrator/assessor	Retailer/marketing staff Consultants and evaluators	

(Based on Jarvis, 1995a, p 186)

those times when they are able to conduct their research or assist the learners who work with them, there is profound satisfaction.

Conclusion

There is a major paradox is this situation: a greater emphasis is being placed on learning and knowledge for a greater proportion of the population than ever before, and yet the academic staff in the institutions of higher education and learning are reporting stress and the users of a great deal of that knowledge are suggesting that the educational system is unable to cope with the demand. When supply and demand do not meet in the market, then new suppliers emerge that seek to respond to it – this we are beginning to see with private universities, corporate universities and even universities of the third age. Opportunities to innovate and respond to more of the demands are still there, but much greater investment in the universities is required for them to be realized.

Change, then, presents both opportunities for development and more cautious reactions that do not always greet it with enthusiasm. The forces for change are coming from outside of the university system (as well as from some voices within it), and so it is now necessary to examine the external forces in order to understand the stresses to which the system is exposed. In a sense, the remainder of this book is an attempt to trace the changes in society that have led to the crisis in the university system, as we know it today, and to raise questions about the way that higher education is currently developing.

2

Globalization and its implications

In order to understand the crisis in universities, it is necessary to look beyond their doors to the changes in the wider world. Universities are not immune from the wider forces of social change, so that studies of the university system that look no further than education itself, or even national policies, are artificially restricting the field of their analysis. Consequently, this chapter examines the processes of globalization, especially economic globalization, as containing the main driving forces of social change. Economic globalization affects both the sovereignty of nation states and their internal policies – especially welfare ones. The chapter, thereafter, examines how these relate to the higher education system. Finally, as social theorists have recognized for many years, the global must be examined in relation to the local, so the final section of this chapter is concerned with 'glocalization'.

The processes of economic globalization

In this section we will look at the globalization process and its effects on the universities. The section has three main parts – the first examines globalization itself and notes how it is not a value-free process but one that has moral implications; the second and third sections look at the opportunities and the problems presented to the universities by these economic and market processes.

Globalization

Globalization (see Beck, 2000 for an introduction to these processes) has become a buzzword in contemporary society and in so doing it has partially replaced the modern/postmodern debate; late modernity is in any case one of the products of globalization. Globalization is a complex phenomenon with many books having been written about it, especially from the early 1990s onwards (see Albrow and King, 1990; Friedman, 1994; Robertson, 1992, *inter alia*).

The process as we know it today began in the West (the USA followed by Western Europe) in the early 1970s, although it can be traced back in history far longer. Beck (2000) makes the distinction between 'globality' and 'globalization'. The former refers to the fact that we have been living in a world society for a considerable period of time; many of the references to globalization and higher education actually refer to this aspect of globality (Blight *et al,* 2000; Scott, 1998). The latter means 'the *processes* through which sovereign national states are criss-crossed and undermined by transnational actors with varying prospects of power, orientations, identities and networks' (Beck, 2000, p 11, emphasis in the original). Both of these points have profound implications for education, especially since one of the major ways by which nation states are undermined is through information technology and the ease with which a great deal of information is transmitted around the world. As a result of these processes, Beck (2000, p 11) makes the significant point that now 'nothing which happens on our planet is only a limited local event'.

In the early 1970s there were a number of contributory factors to the emergence of globalization as we know it today. Among these are: the development of sophisticated information technology through the Star Wars programme, resulting in the Internet; the economic competition from Japan; the GATT agreement and deregulation; and the oil crisis that dented the confidence of the West. Corporations began to examine ways in which they could become more competitive to cope with these factors. They did this by such means as merging and becoming larger in order to be more efficient, and by relocating manufacturing and transferring capital around the world, seeking the cheapest places and the most efficient means to manufacture, and the best markets in which to sell their products. This resulted in a decline in manufacturing industries in parts of the first world and, subsequently, the emergence of new occupational structures.

During this period theorists also first began to suggest that there was actually a world economy based on the capitalist system of exchange. It is inappropriate to explore the various theories of economic globalization in any depth here, but Weede (1990) has isolated three: Galtung's (1971) 'structural theory of imperialism', Wallerstein's (1974) 'world system approach' and Bornschier's (1980) idea of 'investment dependence'. In a fundamental way they all relate to the power of the economic institution and its effects on the whole world. This economic process has become even more potent because of the tremendous advances in technology, especially information technology. The information technology revolution took off during the same period, with one development leading to another, as Castells (1996, p 51f) demonstrates. He argues that 'to some extent, the availability of new technologies constituted as a system in the 1970s was a fundamental basis for the process of socio-economic restructuring in the 1980s' (1996, p 52).

Now the worldwide substructural driving force of social change is technology, especially information technology, driven by those who control capital – both financial and intellectual. From an oversimplistic perspective, this can be understood as thinking of the *world* as having a complex substructure and a complicated superstructure, whereas in the simple Marxist model of society each *society* had its own substructure and a superstructure. For Marx, the substructure was the ownership of the means of production and the superstructure everything else, but this formulation was soon outdated by the creation of the joint stock company, which is now part of the mechanism transforming capitalism itself. Now the substructure is the control of capital, which is more than just financial capital since it also includes intellectual capital, essential for the knowledge society, and the use of this capital facilitated by the control of information technology. In this type of society, transnational corporations are being forced to develop even more knowledge-based commodities in order to compete in this global market, which is resulting in an ever-increasing speed of change in the nature of knowledge itself. Hence, the educational institution whose business has traditionally been knowledge is almost directly exposed to these social pressures for global change, which is changing the nature of education itself.

The substructure has changed from ownership to control, and from wealth to economic and intellectual capital and information technology. Now the superstructure of the globalized world includes the state, work, culture, leisure and so on. However, it must be recognized that the substructure does not completely determine the nature of the superstructure; while there are homogenizing tendencies, for instance, 'McDonaldization' (Ritzer, 1993) there are also fragmenting tendencies (Bauman, 1995). The state, for instance, still plays an important, but restricted role, in global society, but it is no longer sovereign over its own territory. Transnational corporations have already grown so large and powerful that even governments as powerful as the British one have to go 'cap in hand' to the large corporations (like Ford) with requests and financial inducements to them to keep their manufacturing in Britain. But if the corporations decide otherwise, there is little that governments are able to do to persuade them to change their policies, except to offer even larger inducements. Indeed, we have seen the legal battle of the superstate (USA) and the super-corporation (Microsoft) going on for years now and if the superstate cannot defeat the super-corporation, the implications are considerable for the whole world. Beck (2000, p 2) states that this:

means that corporations, especially globally active ones, can play a key role in shaping not only the economy but society as a whole – if 'only' because they have it in their power to withdraw the material resources (capital, taxes, jobs) from society.

Bauman (1998a, pp 66–67) in support of this position, cites the economic calculations of Passat who showed that in 1997, 'No state can resist for more than a few days the speculative pressures of the "markets"'. More significantly, the transnational corporations have been able to locate jobs wherever it has been most beneficial to them throughout the world, creating an international division of labour and generating a global competitive market. Additionally, they are able to locate themselves in countries where they have to pay fewer taxes, so that they underplay their responsibility to the world, although they widely publicize their charitable acts in each country. Certainly the power of the state is in decline and many employers are disentangling themselves from their responsibilities to the welfare state in the countries in which they have located themselves, or even to their own employees (although some do have share option schemes, etc, for their employees).

For Marx, the market was the mechanism of wealth production and power but in globalization, the competitive market becomes the mechanism for corporate growth and dominance, as well as individual wealth. The market mechanism produces winners and losers – but so does every form of competition. Indeed, the standard of living of many people in the developed world has increased considerably; they have better health care, better accommodation, higher quality food, more wealth, better educational opportunities, more leisure and so on. To 'leave it to the market' (in Lady Thatcher's famous phrase) is to generate success – though not always on merit – but also to create failure. Korton (1995, p 83) writes:

> The freedom of the market is the freedom to make money, and when rights are the function of property rather than personhood, only those with property have rights. Furthermore, by maintaining that the only obligation of the individual is to honor contracts and the property rights of others, the 'moral' philosophy of market liberalism effectively releases those who have property from the obligation to those who do not. It ignores the reality that contracts between the weak and the powerful are seldom equal, and the institution of the contract, like the institution of property, tends to reinforce and even increase inequality in unequal societies.

Those who succeed have to invent a discourse of meritocracy, as Bourdieu (1973, p 84) illustrated:

By making social hierarchies and the reproduction of these hierarchies appear to be based upon the hierarchy of 'gifts', merits, or skills established and ratified by its sanctions, or, in a word, by converting social hierarchies into academic hierarchies, the education system fulfils the function of legitimation which is more and more necessary to the perpetuation of the 'social order' as the evolution of the power relationship between classes tends more completely to exclude the imposition of a hierarchy based upon a crude affirmation of the power relationship.

This is a function that education has often performed in the past; but now the global discourse continues to illustrate something of the hollowness of the claim that 'success' in the world is due to merit. But as the plight of the socially excluded is well known, another discourse emerges and they are categorized as 'lazy', 'work-shy', unwilling to 'get on their bikes' and go and find a job. But in almost every government document about education and learning, the plight of the socially excluded is recognized and while there are some efforts to reach them, it is often far too little and far too late. Despite all these pleas for wider participation in education by the excluded, inequality is a symbol of capitalism itself – as Bauman (1998a, p 79), quoting Jeremy Seabrook (1988, p 15), reminds us: 'Poverty cannot be "cured", for it is not a symptom of the disease of capitalism. Quite the reverse: it is evidence of its robust good health, its spur to even great accumulation and effort.'

The rich get richer and the poor and socially excluded get poorer and, a frightening prospect, the socially excluded are becoming redundant to the global economy – especially those from third world countries. Indeed, it seems that even the United Nations is determined to help the rich at the expense of the poor. Monbiot noted in *The Guardian* newspaper (31 August 2000, p 18) that:

The UN (United Nations). . . appears to be turning itself into an enforcement agency for the global economy, helping western companies to penetrate new markets while avoiding the regulations which would be the only effective means of holding them to account. By making peace with power, the UN is declaring war on the powerless.

Writers like Bauman (1998a, 1998b, 1999) are highlighting these social and ethical problems. At the same time, public demonstrations against global capitalism and in support of the cancellation of third world debt are occurring on the streets of London, Washington and Seattle.

But while this is happening, the corporate world continues to gain power. It is also influencing both the initial and the adult and higher education systems, orientating their curricula towards work and away from the humanities. The discourse that school prepares young people for work rather than adulthood is now assumed, as is the one that continuing professional education is the main function of adult and higher education. It must be conceded, however, that this is not a completely new phenomenon since education has never been free of state domination, which in its turn has functioned in support of the traditional capitalist system for many years (Althusser, 1973; Bourdieu, 1973; Bowles and Gintis, 1976, *inter alia*). More recently, Giddens (1998, pp 109–10) made the point that education is not able to reduce the inequalities in society. In addition, as we have already noted, the power of the state is declining in this new global society.

Not all theorists think that the substructural forces of economic globalization determine the shape of the superstructure, although they still recognize that these forces are dominant. Robertson (1992, 1995) for instance, has been concerned to show that globalization is a cultural phenomenon and that it relates closely with the local, while Castells (1996) has argued that the state still has a place to play in a not completely free global market. While Castells is right, it is still clear that the state is losing a great deal of power as globalization occurs.

Nevertheless, this situation has created both opportunities and problems for the universities: opportunities include global cooperation between universities and problems include the idea that universities can be independent forces for democracy in any country.

Opportunities provided for the universities by globalization

Academia has always demanded an international base and as early as the 1950s, when Gouldner (1957–58) discussed the distinction between locals and cosmopolitans; professionals – including academics – fitted the cosmopolitan category. Their orientation was towards the wider world of the profession and not to the narrow world of the bureaucratic organization in which many of them worked. Indeed, my own research in the 1970s (Jarvis, 1977) showed that those with a professional work ideology had lower job satisfaction and greater role strain in bureaucratic organizations while those with a bureaucratic work ideology had a higher job satisfaction in the same types of organization. Paradoxically more professional continuing education for individuals in such organizations might result in a lower job satisfaction because the organizational procedures can inhibit professionals from performing their role in the way that they think they ought. However, it should be recognized that organizations do need both professional and bureaucratic orientations in order to survive successfully. To function efficiently, universities need those academics who find fulfilment and satisfaction in administration nearly as much, but not quite as much, as they need the academics who produce and disseminate knowledge. At the same time, it might be seen that the internationalization of academia presents many opportunities for those who pursue their professional interests.

Indeed, we can see how many academics welcome this aspect of global society: they have done so through the programmes sponsored by the European Union – Erasmus, Grundtvig, Socrates, the Framework research programmes, and so on. These programmes have brought together academics and students from different universities in different countries, who have been able to work together, in some cases, for a number of years. They have created networks of staff across Europe that have subsequently developed other forms of cooperation in a variety of ways. As electronic means of communication continue to become more efficient, possibilities for networked university departments increase, resulting in shared teaching through video-conferencing and other facilities, and so on. Indeed, one of the future models for the university might well be a networked university system, linking departments with similar academic disciplines in different countries in a complementary manner, since few departments are now large enough to span the breadth of the fields in which they are involved. Globalization enables universities to compress time and space, as Harvey (1990) argued, in the pursuit of many of their academic activities in both teaching and researching.

In addition, formalized global networks are already emerging with Universitas 21 being the most well known outside the USA. It is a consortium that initially consisted of 16 universities – four from each of the UK, the USA, Asia and Australasia – although the report on borderless education (CVCP/HEFCE, 2000, p 14) suggests that there are now 23 universities involved. In a similar manner the National Technical University in the USA brings together consortia of universities. This type of arrangement, where universities can maximize their strengths through cooperative working, including academic fellowships and exchange of staff, is another way in which the university system might develop in the future. Indeed, Universitas 21 has already begun to explore ways in which it can enter partnerships with telecommunications companies to offer programmes prepared by these universities globally (Greenhaigh and Maslen, 2000). As this book was being completed, Goddard (2000b) reported that Universitas 21 had reached an agreement with Thomson Learning (a subsidiary of the international publishing corporation) to offer MBAs online in e-commerce and information management. Alan Gilbert, Vice Chancellor of Melbourne University and Chair of Universitas 21 said that 'U21 brings brand, quality assurance and accreditation. Thomson Learning brings a unique capacity in assessment and capacity to solve problems in admissions. Thomson Learning is also a major supplier of high quality content' (cited from Goddard, 2000b). Even so, Meister (1998, p 184) reports that for the corporations, 'the prestige of the academic partner or the "Ivy League Factor", ranked last on their list of criteria. Our survey reinforces the interest among corporate university deans to look outside traditional academic circles to locate flexible and responsive learning partners'.

Universities have also gradually recognized that they can expand their areas of interest and market their programmes worldwide, especially those that are offered in the English language. Hence, the multi-site university is developing, with some universities having offshore campuses. These possibilities have grown with the development of information technology, so that on-line education throughout the world is now a major possibility and universities are enrolling students who no longer attend their campuses, or even visit their countries. Universities are no longer completely located in a single place and their courses are not taught according to a regular timetable – both space and time have been realigned. Indeed, the whole nature of teaching has changed and much of it has become depersonalized. Now learning is becoming more significant than teaching, and writing, design and formatting skills as important as lecturing techniques. New skills are required as some of the old ones decline – these opportunities may only be taken up at a cost, as we pointed out in the last chapter.

New forms of university are emerging, some the result of mergers between educational institutions and others as a result of takeovers. This was the process that the corporations began in the 1970s and which is still continuing. Mega-universities have appeared and it will not be long before we see multinational and then transnational universities emerging, although state regulation and control are currently preventing this. Once universities go down this route, they will be reflecting the processes of economic globalization described earlier in this section and then they will be faced with its problems even more starkly than before.

Problems created for the universities by globalization

Globalization, as we have argued above, produces winners and losers. Economic globalization does not only exclude people in the developed world, as the above discussion shows, it also excludes whole nations from the underdeveloped world. Bauman (1999, pp 175–76) summarizes a United Nations' Development Report:

- consumption has multiplied by a factor of six since 1950, but 1 billion people cannot even satisfy their most elementary needs;
- 60% of residents in developing countries have no basic social infrastructures, 33% no access to drinking water, 25% no accommodation worthy of the name and 20% no sanitary or medical services;
- the average income of 120 million people is less than $1 per day;
- in the world's richest country (the USA), 16.5% live in poverty, 20% of the adult population are illiterate; 13% have a life expectancy of shorter than 60 years;
- the world's three richest men have private assets greater than the combined national products of the 48 poorest countries;
- the fortunes of the 15 richest men exceed the total produce of the whole of sub-Saharan Africa;
- 4% of the wealth of the world's richest 225 men would offer the poor of the world access to elementary medical and educational amenities as well as adequate nutrition.

One of the things for which universities have traditionally stood has been the right to speak out about the injustices of the world. Now they are increasingly dependent on the wealth producers in order to survive and are themselves becoming wealth producers. They are losing whatever independence they had from the economic and political system. Indeed, many of the universities' most prestigious awards – such as honorary doctorates – are being given to the men, and occasionally women, who sign, or who might be persuaded to sign the cheque to assist the university in some project or other. It becomes more difficult for them to speak out against the problems created by the transnational companies that provide their funding. Individual academic staff can lose their employment if they speak out against corporations who fund their own institutions, since academic tenure has either been abolished in some countries and is being weakened in others. In a world that demands a moral stance, universities are losing whatever independence they ever had to take a moral stand on crucial issues.

Students are already aware that universities are becoming more entrapped in economic globalization and the power of the transnational companies. In the USA, students have demonstrated against their own university administrations for having university T-shirts and other branded commodities manufactured by corporations that are known to operate 'sweat shops' – and university commodity production is itself a $2.5 billion per annum industry.

Some universities have been forced to change their suppliers. Featherstone (2000) reports how a major transnational corporation cancelled its contract with Brown University after it was forced by students to join the Fair Labor Association; the corporation also cancelled a $30 million grant to the University of Oregon after it joined the Worker Rights Consortium. In instances like these, power is used quite overtly, what Lukes (1974) regards as the first dimension of power. However, his second and third dimensions – the ability to set the political agenda and the ability to benefit as a result of in-built biases in the social system maintained by structured and culturally patterned behaviour, attitudes and so on – are just as relevant to this discussion. In other words, the transnational corporations can assume power simply because society gives it to them.

Universities may still play a moral role in contemporary society, but governments themselves are losing more of their power as society globalizes. Even so, governments still recognize that there is a need for uncommitted experts when it does seek to make pronouncements, and some university academics are used in this capacity. Governments are also recognizing the changing nature of citizenship in the contemporary world, and some research and development projects have been funded in this area, which is indicative that the moral dimension of globalization is being implicitly recognized (see Jarvis, 2001b, forthcoming).

At the same time, universities are being forced to market their programmes (some do so very successfully) and so learning materials have become a commodity to be sold in the global learning market. Universities have become producers and manufacturers of these learning materials, and their students have become clients and consumers. Indeed, there is a sense in some distance learning institutions, like the British Open University, that tutorial, guidance and support opportunities have become rather like an 'after-sales' service. Globalization is changing the nature of education and calling for a redefinition of the university. Naturally we shall return to this later in this study.

The nation state and universities

There is clearly some difference between globalization theorists about the future of the nation state. Beck defines globalization by its decline and Bauman (1998a, pp 55–76) asks what is to follow it. All recognize that the state's power is declining, but Castells still maintains that there is a place for it.

However, the state is not a homogeneous entity and different states operate in varying ways. During the Cold War period, for instance, there was considerable debate about the nature of the state. Philosophers such as Nozick

(1974) argued for a minimal state where individuals were free to exercise their authenticity and rights, whereas Rawls (1971) and other social theorists such as Phillips (1986) imply that there is a need for a stronger state to provide the framework for a just social order. They were not commending a totalitarian state, but a more welfare-orientated society. Since states do actually vary between the strong ones, which continue to offer welfare policies, like the Nordic countries, and the minimal ones that operate more non-interventionist state policies, such as the USA and the UK, we would expect that their response to globalization would differ accordingly. It is, however, clearly in the transnational companies' interests to operate in minimal, or weak, states since there is less regulation.

In looking at the Finnish policies towards education at the turn of the 21st century, we can find a different emphasis on the place of work in education to that found in UK documents. For instance, in a recent policy document looking towards the year 2004, the Finnish government does not mention work:

> Educational establishments will continue to be important places in which to meet and study. Educational establishments will be increasingly open to serve the educational needs of all age groups. Educational establishments will be innovative centres of learning where teachers collaborate with students in developing new pedagogical applications. Educational establishments will have a greater responsibility for preventing social exclusion. The use of networks for tutoring and support will become more frequent. Pupils and students will be especially supported in the transitional phase between different educational levels. (Ministry of Education, 1999, p 25)

Naturally, it might be argued that the Finnish policy is out of touch, or behind the times, although its report on adult education policy (Kuosmanen, 1999) is as much concerned about vocational as it is about liberal education. These two reports together illustrate that governments can still shield parts of the educational system from the forces of the substructure if it falls within their policies to do so. By way of contrast, the Dearing Report (1997, p 13, para 23) on higher education in the UK claimed that:

> the main aim of higher education (is). . . to sustain a learning society. The four purposes which make up this aim are:
>
> ● to inspire and enable individuals to develop their capabilities to the highest potential levels throughout life, so that they grow

> intellectually, are well equipped for work, can contribute effectively to society and achieve personal fulfilment;
>
> ● to increase knowledge and understanding for their own sake and to foster their application to the benefit of the economy and society;
>
> ● to serve the needs of an adaptable, sustainable, knowledge-based economy at local, regional and national levels;
>
> ● to play a major role in shaping a democratic, civilized and inclusive society.

In this report, which discusses its high ideals for higher education, we can see that there is also a close relationship between higher education and the world of work. We are not being unrealistic here, since we both recognize the significance of this relationship and consider that there should always be a partnership arrangement between them – but partnerships are rarely between equal but different partners. However, the different emphasis in the policies of the two countries is self-evident.

Even in countries that have adopted a more minimal state policy, the universities are still directly influenced by the state's educational policies – or at least by governmental strategies. Griffin (1999, pp 438–40) nicely argues that there is a fundamental difference between national policies and government strategies: policies suggest control while strategies imply endeavours to influence the more powerful or the market. Griffin maintains that it was only during the period of the welfare state that public policy for adult education was possible, and in contemporary society we should be recognizing government statements in terms of strategy. While he was writing about lifelong learning, his argument holds good for a great deal of higher education as well, since higher education institutions are now being forced to earn an increasing amount of their income.

Despite the changes that are occurring, governments can still have some policies about higher education because they still contribute to the funding, although there are times in which they also endeavour to influence the universities strategically. Universities have not always received government funding, as Seville (Seville and Tooley, 1997, pp 22–23) reminds us. He points out that it was only during World War I that the UK government intervened in higher education in earnest and only after World War II that the state took over responsibility for the full funding of universities – something which lasted throughout the heyday of the welfare state in the UK – from 1946 until 1979. However, as part of the dismantling of the welfare state government deliberately reduced its funding for higher education. This reduction has continued as mass higher education has been extended and, consequently, the government is now in a position where it can determine some policies, but much of the time it is in a strategic partnership with higher education.

As the funding has been reduced in the UK, some scholars have argued that higher education could operate without state support. Tooley (1996) for instance, has extended this argument to the whole of the educational system. Naturally, it is possible to look back to historical examples of this, but society was very different in the early part of the 20th century, when universities were not so dependent on the state, to what it is today. It is highly unlikely that they would be able to perform their traditional roles in contemporary society without some financial support. Nevertheless, at the time of writing (2000), the Conservative Party in the UK suggested a variation on this theme, with the state endowing universities with a one-off capital grant large enough to make them both private and independent of the state. However, since the state could not afford to endow all the universities to be independent of the global capitalist system, the proposal was no more that a kite-flying exercise that was not warmly received by many people in the educational system.

Since the early 1980s, universities have increasingly become money earners, but most people still regard them as part of the public educational system and feel that they do have a public responsibility. They have a role to play as partners with the state, so that they should not be entirely subservient to the demands of the market. As part of this partnership the British Prime Minister can claim that education is the best economic investment that we have. Consequently this should allow universities to act in at least a semi-independent manner that should still enable academics to stand back from the economic processes and analyse them independently. This does not, of course, obviate all the problems with being even partially dependent on large corporations that we mentioned above. With the emergence of the European Union, which might operate in a similar manner to a strong state, universities may get more opportunities to function beyond the confines of the market, and even to be critical of some aspects of the globalization processes within which they are entrapped. However, universities are not only global and international organizations; they are nearly all geographically situated and have local regional responsibilities.

The university and its region

As we pointed out above, the world is not becoming totally homogeneous, or McDonaldized; there is also a process of fragmentation that is exacerbating the differences that already exist in the cultural practices of the peoples of the world and in the histories and laws of different states. While some of these differences are being subsumed within the global process, others are being exacerbated. Indeed, large corporations alter their marketing strategies to conform to some of these unique cultural forms. Therefore, difference is as significant to our discussions as convergence. Universities might be obliged to respond to the demands of global forces, but most of them also have a place in the local community; they are in and are an integral part of a local region. Localities are different from each other and universities need to recognize the local space. Indeed, how universities respond to the global will affect the local in a variety of ways, from the type of academic staff who are employed in the university to the local services that the university both requires and can render. In the same way, the local affects the global since local projects, for instance, may gain global recognition, and so on – there is an interrelationship between them.

It is this social process which Robertson (1995) calls 'glocalization'. He emphasizes the fact that the world is interdependent, that local cultures are significant and are constantly being reconstructed. There is often a sense of borrowing ideas and practices from one place or another – we can see how this process occurs in international conferences, networked departments and so on. Since most universities are situated in and are part of their region and its culture, they are also part of its social capital.

Social capital is a problematic concept. According to Fukuyama (1995, p 26) it is 'a capability that arises from the prevalence of trust in a society or in certain parts of it'. He goes on to point out that it is usually transmitted through cultural mechanisms 'like religion, tradition or historical habit'. The problem with this approach is that the social capital is just assumed to exist and it is then transmitted – individuals are consumers of it rather than part of its creative process. Coleman (1990, p 304), by contrast, suggests that social capital is 'created when the relations among persons change in ways that facilitate social action'. In a sense social capital is embodied in relations between people and it cannot be exchanged since it is not the property of individuals but is an attribute of the local community in which people are embedded. Baron *et al* (1998, p 56) offer a slightly different formulation, close to the one put forward by Coleman, when they suggest that 'social capital is a process in which social relations are formed and reformed with material consequences'. Their own research was with people having learning diffi-culties; they discovered that when these individuals were introduced into the workplace it brought to the surface 'a moment when the usually hidden nature of social capital is made apparent'. In their research, the social capital is in the community of the workplace rather than the local community, but then it is something that exists between people. Schuler (1997, p 118) indicates a third approach, in the work on Putnam (1996, p 117) who suggests that social capital is 'the features of social life – networks, norms and trust – that enable participants to act together more effectively to pursue shared objectives'.

A number of things emerge from this discussion: Coleman (1990) makes the point that social capital is created when relationships between people change and Baron *et al* demonstrate that social capital is only a potential until a catalyst, in their case people with learning difficulties, releases it, so that universities are not only part of the potential local social capital, they can play a significant local role in generating it in their educational role. However, any form of capital is only useful if it is invested, so that without conscious involvement in the region, the social capital of universities remains only a potential. What is also clear from these definitions is that nobody owns social capital as a whole although different agencies own some of it; it is a common good, and it is created actively by people and organizations in relationship and it is transmitted through local culture. It cannot be taught in formal education but it can be gained through it, and it can be learnt through the practical processes of daily and social living. It is created, learnt and experienced in social relationships in the community. It exists in the non-formal and informal processes through which people learn, enter other relationships, get involved in social action and are enriched while they help enrich the community. It is about service in the local community, something that was emphasized in the UNESCO (1998) world conference on higher education report, which stated that:

- The traditional missions of higher education systems (to educate, undertake research and provide services to the community) are still valid, but we affirm that their main mission nowadays is to educate responsible citizens, providing an open space for higher education and for learning through life (para 2).
- Higher education is part of a seamless system, starting with early childhood and primary education and continuing through life (para 5).

Trying to involve universities in their regions has always been a concern of university adult educators; the Russell Report (1973) was concerned with precisely the same thing. The service tradition has never been prevalent in the British university system, as it has elsewhere, so that it is hardly surprising that the recommendations of Russell were never implemented. Thornton and Stephens (1977, p 182) pointed out that the 1973 Carnegie Commission report on higher education, *The Purposes and Performance of Higher Education in the United States: Approaching the Year 2000,* includes among the roles of the academic: 'Service – advice and instruction to persons and organizations external to the campus', plus 'Cultural advancement – provision of informational facilities and personnel'. They go on to cite Crossley (1976) who highlighted the fact that it was assumed that the activities of the college or the university would be relevant and useful to the local community. Indeed, among the traditional list of activities for American academics is 'teaching, research and service', whereas it is more likely to be 'teaching, research and administration' in the UK.

However, as we have already mentioned, with the advent of monetarist economics, the idea that education is a service is disappearing and we have all been caught up in trying to sell our educational programmes and expertise in the global learning market. Even so, it must be emphasized that many universities do play very active roles in their local regions, although it brings little or no academic status, staff are rarely allocated time for it and it has no equivalent to the research or the teaching quality assessment exercises. The local place is probably much more central to the idea of higher education in some other countries than it is in the UK. But we are beginning to see partnerships between universities and colleges of further and higher education in the UK that can provide the same type of lifelong learning model. Universities do have a significant role to play at local, regional and national level, as well as on the global scene – they are 'glocal' institutions and need to tailor some of their activities accordingly. They have to respond both to the homogenizing and the fragmenting tendencies of globalization and create a new sense of interrelationships between their activities. No wonder that many who work in universities feel that they are in crisis.

Conclusion

Globalization has resulted in the universities finding new roles and exciting opportunities, but it has also confronted them with new dilemmas and paradoxes, including those of a moral nature. The crisis and stress discussed in the previous chapter are quite understandable – but so too are the job satisfaction and excitement experienced by many academics. Academics in universities are now part of a larger knowledge-based workforce in which they can play a relevant role. However, the problem is that if universities get too sucked into the global systems that are emerging they will no longer be free to be a potent force for democracy in a global economic market system that is certainly not democratic.

That academics are now able to play a relevant role in a knowledge-based workforce also indicates that universities have lost their largely monopolistic role as producers and disseminators of knowledge, but it also indicates that they do have a major place in the global economy. Globalization and the competitive market have generated a massive growth in the knowledge industries that are having profound effects on society and on the universities themselves. The next chapter examines the knowledge society and the nature of knowledge itself in this apparently new world.

3

Knowledge and the knowledge society

At the heart of the forces of change in contemporary global society lies the control of capital – both financial and intellectual – and the control of information technology. Their separation here is for heuristic purposes only since there is considerable overlap between intellectual capital and information technology. This overlap is about knowledge. Some societies in the contemporary world have become known as knowledge societies, but there is a major problem with this to which we will return later in this chapter, since knowledge is undefined and in these instances it actually only refers to specific types of knowledge. Traditionally, however, the universities have almost had a monopoly of the creation – through research and scholarship – and dissemination of knowledge. As Newman, in his *The Idea of the University* (1976) has taught us, the end of the university is knowledge. No wonder that the universities appear to be in a crisis situation when their very foundations are being threatened by the changing nature of society itself. Now we talk about knowledge and information societies, as if knowledge were something of the everyday rather than of the apparently reclusive and elite world of the university.

In this chapter we will first make reference to the idea of the knowledge society and thereafter ask questions about the nature of knowledge itself. Clearly there are many different ways of analysing knowledge: knowledge can be divided by its functions, by the manner in which it is legitimated, and even by its speed of change. Knowledge can be created, managed, packaged, disseminated and so on. Each of these ways of looking at knowledge has been discussed by a variety of theorists and their discussion impinges on our analysis of the university in contemporary society.

The nature of the knowledge society

The debates about the rise of the knowledge society began in the 1960s and 1970s when it was recognized that the industrialism thesis (see Kerr *et al*, 1973, *inter alia*) was dated. No longer was industrialism at the heart of society or the driving force of social change. Bell (1973) for instance, suggested that the post-industrial society is a knowledge society. For him, the driving force of social change was knowledge and by the 1980s the new axial principle was 'computer-assisted "theoretical knowledge" universalised by telecommunications' (Archer, 1990, p 107). Archer actually sees this as an information society, and perhaps the difference between information and knowledge was not so significant to her discussion as we shall suggest it to be later in this chapter.

Everything about this new society was related to the realms of knowledge, even to the extent that humankind was remodelled and Archer (1990, p 109) writes: 'The notion of the computer as the extension of human (computational, cross-referencing, retrieval) capacities has been turned around to yield a concept of superior "artificial intelligence"'.

Educational researchers such as Eurich (1990) also regarded the computer as a major means to the knowledge society – she even called it 'the intelligent tutor'. It was, according to some, to be the computer that brought about the ideal society – even educationalists like Husen (1974, p 238) argued that '*educated ability* will be democracy's replacement for passed-on social prerogatives'. He recognized that the knowledge explosion would be fostered by a combination of computers and reprographics and he foresaw the possibility of '*equal opportunities* for all to receive as much education as they are thought capable of absorbing' (p 240). There was a certain degree of uncritical optimism about the birth of the knowledge society since its instruments were to bring about an economy that could provide wealth for the world.

Archer (1990, p 109), however, was very critical of the value being placed on computers:

> Yet the notion of the *superior* capacity of computers has a lot to do with reconceptualizing what it is to be human than with machines having captured the essence of the human mind. For what has been downgraded if not excluded from the latter concept are human abilities for exercising wisdom, judgement, empathy, discernment, responsibility, accountability and self-regulation. (Emphasis in the original.)

Since technology would enable humankind to achieve its desires, morality – indeed, even humanity – was superfluous. But as we argued in the previous chapter, the new global world is still in need of moral values. Implicit in these arguments was an endeavour to generate a dominant discourse for these technological developments (Foucault, 1972). However, the nature of capitalism was one other major factor emphasized in some of those early analyses of the knowledge society where the driving force of change was information technology. Hence, in this analysis we have argued that capitalism utilizes information technology, but it also employs intellectual capital.

Between 1960 and the 1990s, there was a fundamental shift in the nature of employment in societies utilizing knowledge as a major element in the economy. Stehr (1994, p 75) citing OECD workforce statistics shows that in the UK the percentage of the labour force in manufacturing industry fell from 47.7 per cent in 1960 to 27.3 per cent in 1991, but between the same years the percentage of those in the service sector rose from 47.6 per cent to 70.0 per cent. Similar, but not quite so dramatic changes occurred in a number of countries studied by the OECD. Stehr (1994, p 180) also suggests that by 1980, 41.2 per cent of the US workforce were in knowledge-producing activity. While these figures are higher than those suggested by Reich (1991), they are still in agreement that the nature of the workforce has undergone change and, especially in those societies that are commonly referred to as knowledge societies, a large proportion of it is now regarded as knowledge orientated. Knowledge workers are:

> the creators, manipulators, and purveyors of the stream of information that makes up the post-industrial, post-service global economy. Their ranks include research scientists, design engineers, civil engineers, software analysts, biotechnology workers, public relations specialists, lawyers, investment bankers, management consultants, financial and tax consultants, architects, strategic planners, marketing specialists, film producers and editors, art directors, publishers, writers, editors and journalists. (Rifkin, 1995, p 174)

Knowledge societies, therefore, are spending more of their resources on research and development rather than on manufacturing. Intellectual capital is being created – knowledge resides in organizations and in the scientists and other workers who produce it, plus the very organizational structures within which the workers are employed. This is also a form of capital investment from which the controllers of capital and the company shareholders expect financial returns. The employing companies may be regarded as knowledge-intensive companies (Frenkel *et al*, 1999) since creating and processing knowledge is their main activity. In this sense universities are also knowledge-intensive companies, albeit they are usually publicly owned.

In addition, these are societies where experts are utilized – it is the world of the consultant, advising others as a result of expertise apparently gained usually, but not always, through years of experience and study. People are using their own intellectual expertise to further the cause of the employers – workers are human capital and they are the possessors of intellectual capital.

Even so, other writers are keen to separate the service from the knowledge sector. Thompson *et al* (2000, p 125) rightly point out that many in the service sector still work in highly routinized and monitored employment while the '"real" knowledge economy, such as high-tech clusters in biotechnology or advanced electronics, is vital to the contemporary economy, but relatively small in scope and potential for employment growth' (p 137).

In a sense, however, this is a world in which university academics ought to feel at home, and it would be true to say that entrepreneurial academics have made considerable inroads into these high-tech clusters. Even so, there are others working with different forms of knowledge with which universities are less familiar and, as we showed in the opening chapter, this is helping to create problems in them.

It becomes clear from this discussion that there are actually different forms of knowledge, or knowledges, under consideration here and while more of the workforce is working with knowledge – it is with different forms of knowledge. It is significant in much of the discussion about the knowledge society that the nature of the knowledge to which reference is made is frequently assumed, or if it is defined the definition is often inadequate, which is hardly surprising since this is a very problematic task.

The nature of knowledge

Epistemology is a branch of philosophy and no attempt is going to be made here to summarize even its main discussions. However, in pursuing this argument, we will explore some of the different approaches to knowledge since we need to provide a number of different perspectives on it in order to further our understanding of the relationship between universities and knowledge in contemporary society.

In *A Dictionary of Philosophy* (Flew, 1976) three types of knowledge are discussed:

1. *knowledge that* (factual knowledge);
2. *knowledge how* (practical);
3. *knowledge of* (people and places).

Knowledge that is knowledge based on argument or research, so that it is possible to claim that 'x' is a fact. *Knowledge how* is practical knowledge: I know how to do it. There is a sense in which this latter type of knowledge is often confused with *knowledge that* since it becomes shorthand for *knowledge that this is how* it is done. *Knowledge that,* in both of the forms described here, can be taught in a traditional university setting since the knowledge is usually being mediated to the students through the lecture. By contrast, neither *knowledge how* nor *knowledge of* can be taught in this way, since neither can be mediated; this is a point to which we will return below.

We need to ask, what makes these different types of knowledge true? Scheffler (1965) has suggested that knowledge can be legitimated in at least three different ways: rationalistically, empirically and pragmatically.

Rationalist: this form of knowledge is legitimated by reason. Pure mathematics is often the example provided for knowledge of this type; mathematicians need no objectives beyond the problem and no form of proof that is not to be found within its own logic. Philosophical knowledge is another form of knowledge that is legitimated in this way.

Empirical: empirical knowledge relies on the sense experiences; knowledge is true if it can be shown to relate to an empirical phenomenon. Thus, I know that there is something upon which I am sitting – I can feel it and I do not sink to the ground when I sit down. There is a chair here and I know that there is an object here by my sense experience, even though the *idea* of 'chair' is a construction of experience – but the chair is part of the situation. We can have knowledge of a reality beyond ourselves through our senses.

Pragmatic: pragmatic knowledge is also scientific knowledge since its validity rests on experimentation. If the experiment can be replicated, if the findings of the experiment fit the situation or achieve the desired results, then it is valid knowledge. The pragmatist also emphasizes the experimental nature of certain forms of experience: individuals try something out and find that it works, or it fails. For instance, young university lecturers can be told how to lecture but until they have actually done it they do not know that they can do it, and it is only after having done it many times that expertise in lecturing might begin to develop. They find out by doing it and achieving their desired aims. As Heller (1984) points out, this is also the nature of everyday experience and everyday knowledge – we learn by experiment.

All three of these forms of knowledge can become *knowledge that* either when they become established or when the speakers are telling others what they have actually done in the past, and then these can be mediated to another person, or persons. In other words, universities can teach about all of these three forms of knowledge, but their teaching is only *about,* and in a rapidly changing world there is a danger that this form of knowledge can soon become outdated. Universities have to adapt their teaching so that they can incorporate into it other forms of knowledge.

One theorist who recognizes the significance of pragmatic knowledge, but who places it within a phenomenological framework is Tuomi (1999, p 100). He approaches knowledge from a slightly different perspective; he starts with Polanyi (1967) and suggests that if knowledge is the product of knowing, then there are five different forms of knowledge:

1. tacit – unorganized and dynamic meaning relations;
2. focal – conscious organized patterns of meaning relations;
3. articulated – meaning relations sedimented in produced artifacts or expressions;
4. verbal – meaning relations sedimented within a system of concepts;
5. socially legitimized – socially shared conceptual knowledge.

We will return to tacit knowledge below. Tuomi's discussion relates endeavours to overcome all the problems of so-called objective knowledge, which elsewhere (Jarvis, 1999) has been regarded as information, or even data. Tuomi's analysis has a number of strengths, but it can only relate to specific localities; in this sense it is local – it refers to the organization rather than the universal. We can see, therefore, that for him teaching is a sharing of knowledge that works for those who can use it in the specific locality. He describes what Bourdieu (1990) called the habitus. However, he still omits discussion on the speed of change of knowledge. But, as we mentioned in the opening chapter, this was a concern that Scheler ([1926] 1980) had many years before when he began to raise questions about the relativity of knowledge within the context of a sociological study of culture. From a phenomenological perspective he located knowledge in language and he then tried to distinguish different forms of knowledge by what he regarded as their artificiality, that is their lack of 'embeddedness' in their culture.

As we pointed out in the first chapter, Scheler ([1926] 1980, p 76) suggested that there are seven types of knowledge, and although they are no longer precisely valid, the crux of his position remains acceptable; the revisions to the typology that can be made would, if discussed here, only interfere with this argument. His seven types are:

1. myth and legend – undifferentiated religious, metaphysical, natural and historical;
2. knowledge implicit in everyday language – as opposed to learnt, poetic or technical;
3. religious – from pious to dogmatic;
4. mystical;
5. philosophic–metaphysical;
6. positive knowledge – mathematics, the natural sciences and the humanities;
7. technological.

Scheler regarded his final two forms of knowledge as artificial. There are two reasons for their artificiality – their speed of change and their special, abstract language, which meant that people had to learn a special language in order to master the knowledge. Scheler's was an early attempt to raise fundamental questions about the relativity of knowledge; indeed, he suggested that positive and technological knowledge changed 'hour by hour' – even in the 1920s! He recognized, however, that this artificial knowledge was not embedded in the culture of the people; something that has become even more obvious in contemporary society. In the contemporary global society, a great deal of knowledge never gets embedded in the local culture before it becomes out of date. Indeed, it becomes so complex that we can talk about expert systems in which we have to trust because we can understand neither the way they operate nor the reasons why they do the things that they do. It follows from this, as Scheler recognized, that this artificial knowledge is much more universal than the other forms of knowledge; implicit in this analysis is an understanding of global and local knowledge. Indeed, this artificial knowledge has become one basis of some forms of content knowledge, or traditional theory, which themselves change as a result of research. As we shall claim below, this is one element in practical knowledge, but until the practitioner has tested it in practice it remains information.

This concern for the global and the local is one to which 'glocalization', introduced in the previous chapter, refers. As capitalism has spread throughout the world, and with it the ideas of modernity, it is hardly surprising that positive and technological knowledge is what Bell (1973) regarded as universal knowledge. Indeed, it is the knowledge of globalization. What is clear from this discussion, however, is that there is not a single phenomenon called 'knowledge' that may be regarded as the truth. Lyotard (1984) suggested that all knowledge is narrative and increasingly legitimated by performativity, although he later (1992) modified his assertion and claimed that much knowledge is legitimated by this principle; we will return to this in the following section of this chapter. Foucault also located knowledge in language, but he regarded it as discourse and the dominant discourse was taken as knowledge. However, that discourse is socially constructed. Foucault in *L'ordre du discours* (Sheridan, 1980, p 121) notes how this process occurs:

> In any society the production of discourse is at once controlled, selected, organized and redistributed according to a number of procedures whose role is to avert its powers and its dangers, to master the unpredictable events.

Foucault isolated a number of principles of exclusion – taboo, rejection and so on. In his understanding of the nature of discourse, he outlined one of the major reasons for the growth and development of educational systems – the human will to discover truth rather than knowledge being truth. Sheridan (1980, p 123) commenting on Foucault's analysis of discourse, writes:

> The truth does not impose itself on a pure, receptive mind: it is sought after. Each of the great mutations of scientific knowledge, those of the early seventeenth or nineteenth centuries, for example may be seen as the new forms of the will to truth; new arrangement of the objects to be studied, new functions and positions of the knowing subject, new material investments in the pursuit of knowledge. There is a whole institutional base on which the will to truth operates: the educational system, the distribution of information through libraries, learned societies, laboratories, the values set by different social systems on different forms of knowledge.

With the advent of globalization, we see a dominant discourse about the value of technological knowledge, and about those other elements of global capitalism – efficiency, competitiveness, profits and so on. Consequently, we can begin to see the way in which this discourse is seeking to colonize the world, and how some branches of the university are able to work with the knowledges required by the forces of globalization, while others are not.

Prior to the Enlightenment, the churches founded the universities and this formulation would not have been valid since universities in the West concentrated on the philosophical and the humanities – there was not a great deal of science or technology taught. After the Enlightenment, universities had to adapt and increase the range of subjects taught, and new universities were established, some offering the whole range of subjects including the 'new' sciences, but some others concentrated on the new forms of knowledge – science and technology. Ultimately the complexities of knowledge led to a fragmentation within the university as a community, since different segments of the university pursued different branches of knowledge.

But, as we argued in the last chapter, this global knowledge does include the local, which Robertson (1995) emphasized by using the term 'glocalization'. Local *cultural* knowledge is contained in Scheler's first four forms of knowledge above. However, the socially excluded also have their discourses excluded from the universal knowledge. Even their language is regarded as irrelevant by those who frame the discourse of transnational corporations. Korton, for instance, tells of how the chief executive of Pfizer Inc (a large drugs and medical company) on receiving an award for his contribution to global education, shared his thoughts with several hundred American educators. Korton (1995, p 111) writes that he told them that:

> the education of young Americans must focus on giving them the greatest competitive edge in the new global economy. In his view, there was no time for unnecessary frills – such as studying foreign languages. He reported that in his travels around Pfizer's world operations, he found that everyone with whom there was need to talk already spoke English. So he advised that the classroom hours that children in other countries spend in learning English be devoted to teaching American students science and economics.

Here we see the significance that the transnational corporations actually put on these local forms of knowledge and the high importance placed on the others. The global forces of capitalism might be creating the conditions where there is a standardization of university provision, because this is what some chief executives of the transnational companies expect from them. But there is local, or indigenous knowledge (IK) and universities should see themselves playing a role in the local, as well as in the global.

IK in all cultures is very important and even these drug companies are discovering that folk knowledge and herbal remedies sometimes contain more than a little very valid knowledge, learnt pragmatically over the centuries, as they develop folk remedies into modern money-earning drugs. To destroy IK is to destroy many generations of learning, albeit in different ways and emphases and with different formulations of knowledge to our own. IK is defined by Warren (1991, World Bank Web) as:

> knowledge that is unique to a given culture or society. IK contrasts with the international knowledge system generated by universities, research institutions and private firms. It is the basis for local-level decision making in agriculture, health care, food preparation, education, natural-resource management, and a host of other activities in rural communities.

This is pre-modern knowledge of folk cultures, mostly of the third world, but it is also local knowledge everywhere, such as that of the indigenous peoples of Australia and New Zealand. It is about forms of knowledge not generally considered in discussions about the knowledge society and does not necessarily feature among the priorities of many universities, since much of it is apparently not scientific. Consequently, the modernization project is actually helping to undermine and even destroy local knowledge, although some of it has been attested by the pragmatics of social experimentation. Universities in different parts of the world should have developed, as some have, different programmes to support and research local cultures and to encourage local peoples to understand more fully their own cultures, but this raises problems of funding as we pointed out in the previous chapter.

Universities have traditionally existed to try to discover truth, as well as to disseminate it. Traditionally those endeavours have been contained in language and legitimated through reason and argument, empirically or pragmatically. Lyotard (1984) however, suggested that in this period of late, or post modernity, knowledge would be legitimated through performativity, so that it is now necessary to analyse process and practical knowledge.

Practical knowledge

We have already seen that *knowledge how* cannot be taught in the classroom in precisely the same way as *knowledge that,* although it is possible to adapt teaching techniques to help learners acquire *knowledge how*. But it can be learnt and perhaps shared in practice, which helps explain why mentoring is becoming a major concern for managers in the professions and corporations (Megginson and Clutterbuck, 1995). Professionals' ways of knowing and learning practical knowledge have already been discussed in considerable detail elsewhere (Baskett and Marsick, 1992; Jarvis, 1999) and so we will not repeat it here in detail. However, we want to distinguish between process and practical knowledge. Process knowledge is specifically about *how* the process or the procedure can be conducted and having the skill to do it, whereas practical knowledge is broader and includes such considerations as *why* it should be conducted in this manner, so that the former is a part of the latter. This form of practical knowledge was something that concerned Aristotle many centuries ago. He wrote:

> It follows that in the general sense also the man who is capable of deliberating has practical wisdom. Now no one deliberates about things that are invariable, or about things that are impossible for him

to do. Therefore, since scientific knowledge involves demonstration whose first principles are variable (for all such things might actually be otherwise), and since it is impossible to deliberate about things that are necessary, practical knowledge cannot be scientific knowledge or art; not science because that which can be done is capable of otherwise, not art because action and making are different kinds of things. The remaining alternative, then, is that it is a true and reasoned state of capacity to act with regard to that which are good or bad for man. (Aristotle, 1925 edition, Book VI.5)

We are nearly all aware that both in everyday life and in professional practice, when we understand the situations in which we find ourselves because we have habitualized our behaviour, we do not think about them but can presume on them and act accordingly. No learning occurs. But when we do not know precisely what to do – when there is a gap between what we know and what we need to know, which elsewhere I have called 'disjuncture' – we have to think about it and learn what to do. We have to gain more process knowledge so that we have the *knowledge how*. But for much of our lives we can presume that we know how to act, although if we were to be asked how we did it we might find it hard to explain. It is almost instinctive, or tacit.

Tacit knowledge

Many experienced practitioners have the feeling that 'we can know more than we can tell' (Polanyi, 1967, p 4), which is this tacit dimension. Polanyi instances this by pointing out that we can pick out a face from among a million different ones, but we cannot necessarily describe the person accurately – a form of *knowledge of*. Polanyi recognized that when we focus on specific elements in an experience, we usually see others less consciously but can still give meaning to the whole. This is the tacit dimension to our experience.

In a similar manner, when we habitualize our actions, we might be aware of precisely what we are doing but we often find it difficult, if not impossible, to specify it. Nyiri (1988, pp 20–21) writes:

One becomes an expert not simply by absorbing knowledge of the theory found in textbooks, but through experience, that is, through repeated trials, 'failing, succeeding, wasting time and effort, getting a feel for a problem, learning when to go by the book and when to break the rules'. Human experts thereby gradually absorb 'a repertoire of working rules of thumb, or "heuristics", that, combined with book knowledge, make them expert practitioners'. This practical, heuristic knowledge, as attempts to simulate it on the machine have shown, is 'hardest to get at because experts – or anyone else – rarely have the self-awareness to recognize what it is. So it must be mined out of their heads painstakingly, one jewel at a time'. (All quotes cited from Feigenbaum and McCorduck, 1984.)

Tacit knowledge, then, is developed from experience, either pre-consciously – that is without having ever entered the conscious mind – or else it has been learnt consciously but been forgotten because of our familiarity with the actions that we undertake. It consists both of process and content knowledge that together underlie taken-for-granted practice. How or when we learnt becomes irrelevant; it is stored away and no longer conspicuous in our consciousness. Most importantly, we can presume tacitly, precisely because it does work for us. The very essence of tacitness is pragmatic. When we enter different situations, we are able to call upon depths of taken-for-granted knowledge that we may not be able to articulate. Because it works, we can continue to presume upon it. This tacit knowledge is not only the knowledge of experts: it is present in all forms of practical knowledge.

Schon (1983, p 54) makes similar points about professionals' practical knowledge. He suggests that professionals:

- know how to carry out actions spontaneously;
- are not always aware of having learnt to do these things;
- are usually unable to describe the knowing which the action needs.

Tacit knowledge, then, can occur in *knowledge that, how,* or *of* forms. Since all learning is biographical this tacit dimension is also built into our own biographies and on occasions we all act in a taken-for-granted manner without necessarily being able to articulate the reasons. This is why practitioners sometimes appear to be inarticulate about their practice; they have learnt to take so much for granted, to act on tacit knowledge, that it not longer resides in their immediate consciousness.

Learning practical knowledge

From this discussion we can see that the practice of pragmatism is actually a learning process. The whole of life is, in this sense, based on pragmatic knowledge and we are continually incorporating it into our biography as we learn from life's experiences. However, life's experiences are not value-free, so that our practice also reflects our beliefs or our values. Practical knowledge is, therefore, not neutral knowledge. Indeed, it is more than knowledge in the traditional sense – it is having the skill to undertake the whole role. It is an individual's body of learning about practice. Pragmatic knowledge is learnt, not taught, so that it is something removed from the university's traditional functions. We learn this form of knowledge through direct experience, but we are taught theory through mediated experience and we have to test it out in order to legitimate it for us. However, it would be false to assume that because practical knowledge works, it necessarily provides the correct or even the best way of doing something – it is merely one way to achieve desired ends. Practical knowledge, then, is a combination of different forms of knowledge, and we are now in a position to depict the practical knowledge of practitioners in the manner shown in Figure 3.1.

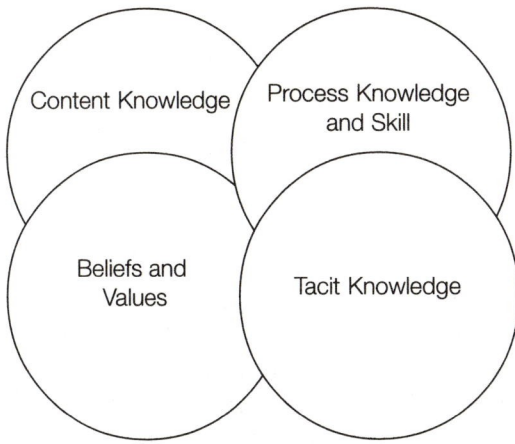

Figure 3.1 The nature of practical knowledge

Practical knowledge, then, is:

- both learnt and legitimated in practice situations;
- practical, and not merely the application of some 'pure' academic discipline to practical situations;
- theoretical in that it contains content knowledge;
- dynamic, in as much as it is only retained for as long as it works;
- integrated, rather than divided up by academic discipline;
- not an academic discipline in the same way as the sciences or the social sciences, although certain practice fields such as education and medicine have claimed to be academic disciplines;
- subjective and not value-free.

It may be seen that this analysis of practical knowledge relates quite closely to what Gibbons *et al* (1994) call 'Mode 2 knowledge'. It is one of the forms of knowledge that is closer to the world of the transnational corporations, which need workers who know what to do and have the ability to do it. It is a form of knowledge and skill that has a short 'shelf-life'. Meister (1998, p 11) suggest that it is relevant for a period as short as 12 to 18 months. However, this approach to knowledge is one that is far removed from the world of the traditional universities that have taught abstract, theoretical knowledge, or content knowledge that has a long period of validity – even universal knowledge. Consequently, these differences call for the university to change and expand its teaching and assessment patterns, but not necessarily to jettison its broader approaches to knowledge, since the position adopted in this book comes close to what Barnett (1994, p 179) called 'reflective knowing'. However, it also requires universities to reconsider the nature of research. We will examine research in two parts, the first in this chapter, and re-examine research into practical knowledge in the following chapter.

Research

In the knowledge economy it would be true to claim that knowledge is money and so the development of new knowledge becomes imperative for those transnational companies whose survival depends on it. But it is obvious that they are really only concerned with scientific and technological knowledge, so that they can develop new products that can be marketed, and those aspects of practical knowledge that enable them to function efficiently. Many universities, in contrast, regard their research function as spanning the whole range of knowledge, although with the fragmentation of the university even this statement is becoming debatable.

Seeking new scientific and technological knowledge is often a very costly enterprise in which universities bid for money from funding councils and other agencies. University academics are frequently driven by the demands of the discipline, or the state of knowledge in a given field, to undertake their research; they certainly have the intellectual capital to undertake the projects upon which they embark. In contrast, the large corporations have the financial capital but, in some instances, they make lack some of the intellectual capital to undertake research, though this is not true of many transnational companies that have their own research and development sections. However, the motives for undertaking the research might vary: academics seeking to understand the problem for the sake of the knowledge itself, while the corporations want the marketable products that might stem from it. This means that once corporations have decided that it is in their best interests to undertake the research project, the capital is made available for undertaking it, either by conducting it themselves or by buying in the research from other agencies, such as universities. This often results in the corporations funding university research projects, as well as their own. Partnerships have become an important development in the research enterprise but, frequently in partnership arrangements, the commercial sponsor claims the right of patent on any new discoveries even though they have been made by university staff.

Universities are major players in the research process, but because of the limitations of their funding, they have often felt weaker than they actually are in the knowledge-driven economy. Consequently, universities have become 'willing' collaborators in the commercialization of their own research, and this actually results in the universities becoming even more market driven. Amit (2000, p 220) makes the point for the Canadian universities that:

> If Canadian governments did not deliberately underfund the post-secondary sector in order to render university administrators and faculty members alike more receptive to commercialization, they have not been averse to capitalizing on the 'persuasive' efforts of their cuts. So we appear to have a quite cynical but apparently straightforward scenario of manipulation and compulsion in which one political hand reduces support for more traditional forms of university activities while the other hand tantalizes with new funding possibilities intended to remodel more fundamental elements of the traditional mission.

From the other perspective we have university managers rewarding academics for obtaining funds from commercial organizations for research, even though it is undermining the relative independence of the universities. While academic freedom has traditionally allowed university researchers to undertake their own research, the question still remains as to whether universities were actually ever truly independent bodies.

Universities have traditionally not sought to exploit their research findings in a commercially productive manner, whereas the large corporations have. Consequently, the ownership of research knowledge becomes an issue in contemporary society. Corporations producing knowledge that might result in commercial products immediately seek to patent their findings in order to gain financial advantage from their research – universities are only just learning to develop their research findings into commercial products. Traditionally their research knowledge has been made public for wider use – which has sometimes resulted in other corporations exploiting it to their own benefit so that the outcome has not been totally free use.

A major problem that emerges from the commercialization of research knowledge is that the patent restricts the use of the knowledge to a single organization that has a monopoly right of use for many years, sometimes longer than the usefulness of the knowledge itself. Large pharmaceutical and other research companies can then, for instance, control drugs and other treatments and sell them, often at inflated prices, which results in the poor of the world not being able to benefit from them as much as they might. This problem is growing as research into the human genetic make-up is under way, with all the possible benefits the developments from this research might provide. Hence we see another of the ethical issues about global capitalism to which reference was made in Chapter 2.

Indeed, these problems are well recognized by some academics themselves, some of whom are claiming that corporate funding in research is becoming unacceptable because it is continuing to erode academic freedom in these matters. The *Chronicle of Higher Education* in the United States has reported how medical schools are demanding that their professors become more aggressive in the pursuit of corporate funding, and even tying professors' salaries to their ability to attract that funding. Perhaps in a less aggressive manner this is also happening in the UK. But there is a reaction:

> Professors. . . are complaining that corporate money comes with too many strings attached. Professors complain that corporate sponsors often decide what will be studied, how the research will be conducted, and under what conditions the results will be published. Conflicts between the secrecy demanded by corporate funders and the traditionally open atmosphere of the academic research community have also led to growing dissatisfaction among university researchers. (*Philanthropy News Digest*, 5, 22, 1999)

One of the great advantages of financial gain is that it provides a powerful motivator for research and development to be undertaken. In addition, it can be argued that the standard of living of those who benefit from the outcomes of research has been enhanced tremendously. Whether the world can be said to be a happier place for everybody is another matter, although it certainly can for those people whose health has been improved as a result of research.

Whether universities should always seek to exploit their research findings in the market is a moral dilemma for them and the more they move in this direction the more they become like private institutions – a form of corporation marketing its knowledge. Clearly many new knowledge-based companies are university inspired and while some of these are actually in private ownership, the universities have got to go down this road in the global economy and create and own market commodities that have been developed from their research. One might hope, however, that their products might be made available at prices more people can afford, since they might have fewer shareholders to satisfy. Universities should be taking the moral high ground in this matter. Paradoxically, the more successful they are in this enterprise, the more influence they can actually assert and the more independent they might actually become – if this is regarded as something integral to the nature of the university itself.

We will return to the subject of researching practical knowledge in the next chapter, when we examine teaching and learning.

Managing knowledge

Senge (1990, p 69) suggests that:

> Perhaps, for the first time in history, humankind has the capacity to create far more information than anyone can absorb, to foster far greater independency than anyone can manage, and to accelerate change far faster than anyone's ability to keep pace. Certainly the scale of complexity is without precedent.

Consequently, it is necessary to try to manage all the information in order that those who require it might access it effectively. McInerney and LeFevre (2000, p 1) state: 'Virtually all large firms that create knowledge management systems use information technology to organize, store and codify knowledge and make it accessible to members.'

A corporation's knowledge resides in all the reports and other documents that it has produced about itself and its activities, and in its staff. Most of the documents are linked together electronically so that appropriate personnel may access them, whenever they require them. The systems that contain the corporation's knowledge and the knowledge workers themselves are the intellectual assets – the intellectual capital – of the corporation or the university. Both are important, and access to the computer system of a large corporation is usually restricted, so that the corporation's knowledge is not public. It is, in some ways, like a private library and its function can be likened to one but, unlike university librarians, the knowledge managers select what is stored in the system. Naturally, they are not neutral: their choices reflect the corporation's interests and concerns. They decide what is to be included, omitted or deleted as obsolete and so on. In other words, they decide what is essential, relevant, or useful knowledge for their company. This is, therefore, much closer to a private library than to a university one.

Consequently, it is of considerable interest and concern that the World Bank devoted 4 per cent of its administrative budget in 1999 to develop a knowledge management system (Stromquist and Samoff, 2000, p 326), since it provides information and advice across the world. Stromquist and Samoff (pp 326–27) report that the World Bank asked academics to provide annotated bibliographies on selected categories of knowledge from which they would construct several databases. They make the following comments on this:

> It is important to note several critical steps here: (1) by selecting the categories the World Bank determined unilaterally which education issues mattered most; (2) by seeking professionals in the North, the World Bank granted greater legitimacy to knowledge produced in the North (and in English); (3) by reducing research knowledge to a few statements, situational conditions and features delimiting research findings were discarded, resulting in knowledge that is fragmented, reduced to its minimum expression, and decontextualized; (4) by working through CIES (Comparative and International Education Society) the World Bank brought instant legitimacy to its project. Notwithstanding the recruitment of senior CIES scholars, the World Bank retained control over the content of the databases, rejecting without explanation several of the abstracts that were prepared.

The World Bank has, therefore, arbitrarily defined relevant educational knowledge, which Stromquist and Samoff suggest 'will emphasize knowledge that is explicitly linked to the economic sphere and that is assumed to have the greatest potential to increase productivity' (p 329). This is one way in which educational knowledge, which will no doubt be used to provide advice and upon which policy will be based, has been constructed. Consequently, we can begin to see how those who have power can determine what knowledge gets into the management system and is subsequently used. Educational knowledge of this type is being created by those who control the global substructure, in the same manner as corporate knowledge is created.

Stromquist and Samoff go on to cast doubts upon the fact that this educational knowledge system will be accessible to everyone. In the same manner, corporations have sought to restrict the use of the knowledge generated by their staff. Even those who work for McKinsey, for instance, have to agree never to disclose confidential information about the company or its clients, even after leaving it (Rastel, 1998, p xiv). Employees of other consulting firms are required to do the same. Essential corporation knowledge is stored on the centralized corporation computer system, often in the USA, and managed from there. Employees from elsewhere in the world access the knowledge network, one of whose staff acts rather like a research librarian/assistant and produces the required information within a specified time, such as two days, for the enquiring branch of the company. Indeed, if it is not forthcoming within that period, it is regarded as poor job performance and recorded as such. Without these intellectual assets, knowledge-intensive companies would not survive. Lyotard (1984, p 5) suggested that:

> Knowledge in the form of an informational commodity indispensable to productive power is already, and will continue to be, a major — perhaps *the* major — stake in the worldwide competition for power. It is conceivable that the nation states will one day fight for control of information, just as they battled in the past for control over territory, and afterwards for the control of access to and exploitation of raw materials and cheap labor. (Emphasis in original.)

It is not the nation states that will engage in the battle but it might be the transnational corporations. Neither industrial espionage nor, in the UK, universities 'poaching' highly qualified academic and research staff for the Research Assessment Exercises are unknown phenomena! Universities act in precisely the same way as other knowledge-intensive organizations.

However, universities have functioned differently in the way that they have managed knowledge. The university library endeavoured to make available as large a collection of books, theses and papers (and now electronic data) as possible to cater for the intellectual interests of all its academics, but it has also served as a public library with access sometimes being offered to local residents as well as scholars. In this sense it has been part of the social capital of the locality. But due to financial stringency university libraries have been cut back and the cataloguing of research reports and theses restricted. This is hardly surprising when we consider the breadth of coverage of knowledge that university libraries have been required to undertake. Universities have been able to offer their intellectual capital to a wider public in the past than they currently can.

Knowledge management is, to some considerable extent, also about managing the people who make up the organization (human resource management). Studies of human resource development and management take us beyond the scope of this chapter, but we will return to them later when we examine the corporate university.

Conclusion

This chapter has deliberately sought to combine discussions about knowledge *per se* and those discussions that reflect the global knowledge economy. It might be argued that the dominant discourse of global society is about knowledge but that this is a deliberately undefined concept since it is more about an ideological discourse than it is about the nature of knowledge itself. In other words, the dominant global discourse is about universal knowledge, about scientific and technological knowledge reflecting the power of the substructural forces of globalization. However, when we sought a broader conceptualization of knowledge, we began to see some of the problems with which the universities are confronted.

Among the first writers who pointed us in this direction were Illich and Verne (1976) who were writing at a time when the French were beginning to introduce laws that made corporations responsible for the education and training of their workforce. This included having to spend 0.8 per cent of their annual budget on education and training although at that time they were actually spending 1.35 per cent (Caspar, 1992, p 149). Illich and Verne claimed that this was money spent on an education and training that the workers neither wanted nor needed, but that it would give the employers a greater control over a workforce that was being made to feel constantly inadequate by the introduction of systems that would also serve a function of providing many more university graduates with employment. They wrote:

> Without doubt, deschooling here falls into a well-concealed trap, laid by those who wish to utilize it to justify the educational megamachine of the year 2000.
>
> With the spread of industrialization of education, and the commercialization of knowledge, it amounts, basically, to bringing back the hidden curriculum of schooling and confirming the obvious consequences. . . a guarantee of our permanent inadequacy.
>
> . . . the semi-skilled worker(s) at the Renault works in Boulogne-Billancourt will be given the clear impression that they have at all times the possibility of climbing the social ladder, with the help of education and training and the educational resources which have been assigned to them. They will have the permanent knowledge that the opportunity to reach the top of the ladder is always there, and that it is entirely due to their own deficiencies if they fail to grasp it. (Illich and Verne, 1976, pp 12–16)

They were clear that this knowledge is one of the foundations of capitalism and that workers were to be 'imprisoned within a global classroom' to learn the necessary knowledge in order to perform their role in society. This approach echoes Archer's analysis of the way that the computer was seen as replacing the human being. This is not a value-free society, neither is the discourse of contemporary society. Many people in the first world have clearly benefited from all the advances that have been made in science, and obviously the potential for the knowledge society to be a universally beneficial society certainly exists. Indeed, it could also be argued that when transnational corporations transfer their manufacturing activities to third world countries, it does help improve the conditions under which many people in these countries live, even though many in the first world consider that the third world is being exploited.

However, the other thing that becomes clear from our analyses of the knowledge society is that this society, where the dominant forms of knowledge are changing and expanding rapidly, is placing considerable pressure on the universities. When universities do not enjoy the wealth to undertake all the research that all the academic disciplines demand, they are forced to respond to the demands of the transnational corporations. Fewer opportunities for research exist in the humanities and local cultural studies. Universities are losing some of their independence in generating new knowledge in the face of the dominant forces of global capitalism.

The rapid changes in knowledge also mean that there must be considerable emphasis on the dissemination of knowledge through teaching and even more on learning. The next chapter examines learning and the following one the learning society.

4

From teaching to learning

Thus far we have seen how globalization is creating rapid social change and the knowledge society. However, it was clear in the previous chapter that a greater emphasis is now being placed on the process of learning knowledge than on teaching it. Traditionally, universities have taught it; in the UK university academics have frequently been referred to as 'university teachers', in the same way as schoolteachers are teachers. They have rarely been referred to as facilitators of learning or, as we have also heard, learning technicians. Indeed, many books about teaching actually spend little time or space on the learning process. Even so, the resistance among academics in universities until just recently to be trained to teach is indicative of the fact that both teaching and learning were considered to be just natural processes that anyone could do if they had the content knowledge. Many programmes on teaching have not been too concerned about how people learn or how knowledge of this should affect the way in which teaching is conducted. Now this is changing. Significantly, this is also the case with company training; in both the focus is now on learning. This has led to ideas about lifelong learning, which we will return to below.

The first part of this chapter looks briefly at the dissemination of knowledge. The next three parts examine the movement from teaching to learning, the processes of learning and lifelong learning; thereafter we examine some of the new approaches to facilitating learning, distance education and, finally, we look at the relationship between learning and research.

The dissemination of knowledge

Universities have traditionally disseminated knowledge through academics lecturing to the students. Lectures were given and frequently neither notes nor handouts were produced for the students; they were expected to learn what they could from the knowledge holder. The academics were employed to disseminate knowledge in a real-time situation that could not be replicated unless the lecturers merely read their notes – which many of them did! But they were the lecturers' notes and not the students', so what the students learnt was an imperfect re-creation of the information provided by the lecturers. Since the lectures were given to students in the university, the dissemination of knowledge was restricted.

In order to disseminate knowledge more widely, universities were among the early founders of book publishing. However, they have never had a monopoly in this field and commercial enterprises have also undertaken the same role. Publishers have worked with university academics, publishing their work and profiting from it. It has been difficult for universities to control this process, even had they wanted to, since the intellectual copyright of that material has always resided with the author of the written word, and only if the author actually assigned the copyright to the university could it be controlled by it. Indeed, it has also been difficult for authors to control their own work and organizations such as The Authors' Licensing and Collecting Society have emerged to help authors gain financial returns from their intellectual property.

When academics are employed by the university specifically to write material for a university course, there has always been a case for recognizing that the employing university should control it and, perhaps, also own its copyright. This problem has always been present when writing books and papers after having completed a research project. Should the research supervisors attach their names to these books and papers, even if most of the work has been undertaken by the students or research assistants whose intellectual copyright it is? Often these agreements are easily worked out, but there are occasions when the research assistants and students have felt that they have been deprived of some of their intellectual rights by their supervisors.

The problem of intellectual copyright remains, and universities have not yet resorted to the same approach as McKinsey in expecting its employees to keep confidential all the knowledge learnt during the period of employment. There appear to be instances emerging, however, where students working with university researchers are being asked to sign confidentiality agreements, assigning either the intellectual copyright of all the knowledge gained or all that gained about the research project to the senior researcher or to the university itself. We can see that if this is the direction in which universities are moving, in restricting the intellectual copyright of academics, then they will have gone further down the road to becoming private corporations and to playing a different role in the knowledge economy.

When radio and television were established the universities did not get overly involved, leaving the business of educating the general public to public broadcasting. Despite the early use of radio in educational innovations in Australia and elsewhere, it was not generally seen as a major educational tool until the foundation of the British Open University. Even here, the printed word occupied the major role and the radio and television programmes were treated as almost optional extras.

With the advent of new information technology, the situation has moved away from the printed word – much of the teaching material is now produced online and universities can now disseminate knowledge across the globe. It is through the dissemination of knowledge, rather than through research, that universities can transform themselves into mega-universities (Daniel, 1996); we will return to this topic below.

Teaching

Universities have traditionally been geared to disseminating knowledge through face-to-face teaching. The university has been located in a specific geographical place and students have had to travel there, often at times convenient to the university, in order to gain access to the knowledge. University academics have lectured and, occasionally, introduced other teaching methods. They have been slow to change from teacher-centred methods. Now different approaches to teaching are being generated and it is more widely recognized that university staff are in need of additional training. However, this is rather like 'closing the door after the horse has bolted', since the emphasis is now as much on learning and the dissemination of knowledge through electronic means as it is on teaching. In the latter, technical experts are now playing a role in course teams in preparing the programmes for use. Academics may only have to produce the knowledge; how it is presented might no longer be their concern.

There are many books on teaching methods (Brown and Atkins, 1988; Jarvis, 1995, *inter alia*) so we will not pursue this any further here. However, there have been a number of indications that changes are occurring in teaching and learning and Jarvis *et al* (1998) have outlined some of these trends as being a move from:

- childhood to adult to lifelong;
- teacher-centred to student-centred;
- face-to-face to distance;

- education to learning;
- the few to the many;
- liberal to vocational;
- theoretical to practical;
- single-discipline to multidiscipline to integrated knowledge;
- knowledge as truth to knowledge as relative;
- rote learning to reflective learning;
- welfare provision (needs) to market demands (wants);
- classical curriculum to romantic curriculum to programme;
- learning as process to learning as content.

In addition, there are problems of assessment. Many of these points have been implicit in the discussions so far and they will occur in the remainder of this book, so we will not elaborate upon them here. The implication of this argument, however, is that universities' dissemination of knowledge should move away from models that emphasize traditional teaching to those that emphasize learning. At the same time, universities teach a variety of types of knowledge, so that traditional teaching methods might well retain an important place in the curriculum. But the role of the university teacher is changing from being the fount of all wisdom prescribing knowledge to being a facilitator of learning. University teachers are being forced to learn new roles and also to be trained in the arts of teaching adults, where many of these teaching methods actually originated. Indeed, Kwan (2000, p 139) commenting on problem-based learning (PBL – see below) says that the 'key is in the re-education and re-training of teachers and rewarding those who accept and engage in PBL'. The focus of the remainder of this chapter, therefore, is on the change from teaching to learning and its implications.

From teaching to learning

In the positivistic society of modernity, researchers have been concerned about end products and their measurement, so that it is hardly surprising that behaviourist theories of learning (see Borger and Seaborne, 1966), emphasizing measurable outcomes, still dominate some branches of learning theory. Even so, this has been modified by the recognition of cognitivist theories that suggest that as we grow towards adulthood our ability to conceptualize alters (Piaget, 1929, *inter alia*). But we had forgotten Kant's claim at the start of his *Critique of Pure Reason*:

> That all our knowledge begins with experience there can be no doubt. How is it possible that the faculty of knowledge should be awakened into exercise than by means of objects which affect our senses, and partly of themselves produce representations, partly rouse our powers of understanding into activity, to compare, to connect, or to separate these, and so convert the raw material of our sense impressions into a knowledge of objects, which is called experience? In respect of time, therefore, no knowledge of ours is antecedent to experience, but begins with it. (Kant, 1934 edn)

Experience is a profoundly difficult subject to analyse, but experiential learning has become the major focus of learning theory. In my own work (Jarvis, 1987, 1992, 1995) and that of many other theorists (Belenky *et al,* 1986; Boud *et al,* 1985; Kolb, 1984; Rogers, 1969; Weil and McGill, 1989, *inter alia*) learning is regarded as an experiential process.

My own research over many years has been into adult learning and I have published various models of the learning processes which relate both to my initial research into it (Jarvis, 1987) and to the continuing developments in the model as I run workshops about the learning processes. Learning is a very complicated set of processes and no diagrams can actually capture all of them. Figure 4.1 illustrates something of the process and represents the latest amendments in my ongoing research into human learning (see page 64). It shows a variety of different learning processes: non-learning, incidental self-learning, non-reflective learning and reflective learning. It represents something of the complexity of human learning, highlighting just some ways in which experience can be created and transformed. Obviously we cannot spend a great deal of time on the diagram and trace all the different routes through it, or even build new ones, since this is inappropriate here, although I do want to trace a few of the processes. (If you wish to follow these points further, see Jarvis, 2001a.)

Nevertheless, before we do this it is necessary to have a clear understanding of what we mean by learning. There have been many different definitions, from behaviourist to more experiential. Behaviourists define learning as 'more or less any permanent change in behaviour which is the result of experience' (Borger and Seaborne, 1966, p 14). However, the change of behaviour is as a result of the learning that occurs through the experience – learning is the process and the change is the product. Since process and product are not synonymous, we can see the logical flaw in this definition. Elsewhere (Jarvis, 1987) I have argued that there are also methodological errors in research of this kind, so that it should be rejected, although we will see in the next chapter how the errors of this approach still persist in attempts at understanding the learning society.

In the research programme into the learning society, Eraut (Coffield, 2000, p 22) produces a definition for the project in which he is involved. For him learning refers to 'significant changes in capability or understanding, and exclude(s) the acquisition of further information when it does not contribute to such changes'.

While Coffield cites this definition with approval, it is actually open to a number of damaging criticisms since:

- 'significant' is something upon which there can be disagreement between people – there is no benchmark and no assessor of significance;
- it actually defines learning by specifically excluding some forms of learning, which is not logically tenable;
- it omits many facets of human learning, such as the emotions and values that constitute our humanity.

It is necessary to have a definition that does not fall foul of these problems. At this stage, I want to offer my own definition of learning, developed from my original research, which is:

Learning is the process of individuals constructing and transforming experience into knowledge, skills, attitudes, values, beliefs, emotions and the senses.

This definition is much wider than the approach to learning traditionally adopted in all universities, including the corporate ones, which restricts it to individual development and career progress and to the corporation's overall capacity (Kenny-Wallace, 2000, p 72).

First of all, we must see that it is people who learn; all learning affects the learners' biography. Despite the nomenclature, it is not societies, nor organizations – but people who learn. Neither is learning a matter of merely storing knowledge passively in the mind: all learning affects the learners' self – note the shadowed boxes in Figure 4.1 (boxes, 1, 3, 4 and 10). Consequently, we do not, for example, teach maths – we teach *people* maths. Learners carry all their previous experiences to their new situations – and that assists them interpret and make sense of their situations, leading to their experiences. Since learning is a matter of constructing and transforming experience into knowledge, skills, attitudes, values, beliefs, emotions and the senses, learners always carry the whole of their biography into every new learning situation.

It must also be observed that at the point that whatever learning is undertaken, whether it is for vocational or non-vocational reasons, the learning still affects the biography so that there are always opportunities for personal growth. Indeed, it could be argued that education for its own sake would not necessarily produce such a demand for formal learning. Work-related

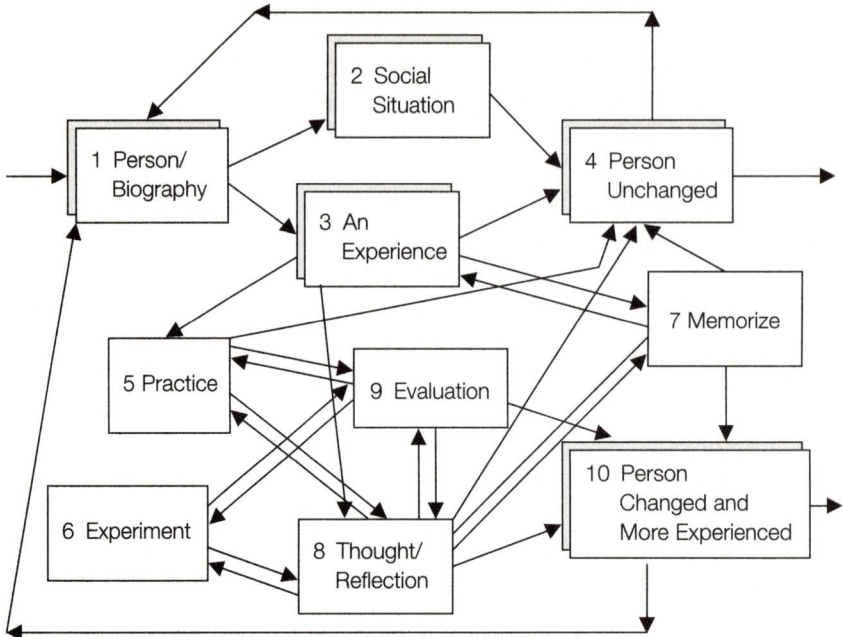

Figure 4.1 A model of the processes of learning

learning can produce very positive biographical outcomes – people grow and develop as persons in these situations even though this may not be the intended outcomes of such planned learning.

Now, we can see how the first part of this definition of learning takes us from boxes 1 to 2 and 3; it is from the actual experience that we learn and we transform it into not only knowledge but skills, attitudes, beliefs, values and so on.

Let us illustrate this from the topic of this book. If we (box 1) are in *the classroom as a student* (box 2) we will in some way experience this situation and be presented with *knowledge that* (box 3) – we may be learning nothing (box 3 to 4), or we may seek to memorize what we are being taught (box 3 to 7), or think and reflect about it (box 3 to 8). Our primary experience is being in the classroom but our secondary experience is of the knowledge with which we are presented. *Knowledge that* is mediated to us – or university teachers are the mediators of *knowledge that*. What we cannot do is go down the route to practice (box 5) because that is not the role of the student sitting in the lecture theatre, so that we cannot actually learn skills. We can only learn skills if we change our role and create a new situation. But if we are *in the lecture theatre as a teacher* (box 2), we have an experience of teaching (box 3), we can practise (box 3 to 5) and even experiment (box 5 to 6) with our teaching skills, but we will inevitably also go down the other routes described above and learn other forms of knowledge simultaneously. In other words, as we are learning to perform or through performing, we are also learning knowledge, attitudes, beliefs, values, etc. It is significant, therefore, that when we learn theory, it is impossible to learn how to do; when we are learning to practise we cannot escape from learning knowledge as well as the skill. We can only learn *knowledge how* to do something if we are also (the learners) practising it.

When we take our situation for granted, whether it is the classroom as student, or the lecture theatre as university teacher, we will move into a non-learning mode (boxes 2 to 4, or 2 to 3 to 4). This is *habitualization*. In professional practice this might occur when practitioners already have sufficient knowledge to respond to the situation, or when their tacit knowledge allows them to presume upon their situation. However, when the student or the teacher cannot take the situation for granted, then a potential learning opportunity occurs. These are situations of *disjuncture*, when biography and experience are not in harmony with each other – when individuals do not have the knowledge, or the skill, or both to take their situation for granted. Disjuncture – knowing that we do not know – is fundamental to our understanding of learning. Significantly, we can conclude that it is mostly in disjunctural situations that we learn, so that if our learning from experience results in too much habitualization we may cease to learn, or if the organizational procedures demand conformity, then there can be no learning resulting in change and development in the organization, although there might be increased dissatisfaction in the learners themselves.

It may be seen from Figure 4.1 that individuals can learn in every situation in which they find themselves throughout their lives. Age is no barrier to learning, although university campuses still cater mainly, almost exclusively in some instances, for the typical undergraduate between the ages of 18 and 25 years.

Lifelong learning

It is important to note that a certain degree of confusion has emerged in the educational vocabulary about the concept of learning: there is an increasing tendency to merge the concepts of education and learning into one – learning. This was to be found quite early in the adult education literature in the USA (see, for example, Long, 1983). Hence, lifelong education and lifelong learning have come to be treated, wrongly in my view, as synonymous in UK government reports (eg, DfEE, 1998a). Education is the institutionalization of learning, and this process can occur at national or at corporate level, as well as at an individual and informal one. Education is about the provision of learning opportunities whereas learning is about consumption. In this sense, education is planned and controlled learning, usually having a curriculum or a programme, and having specified aims and objectives. By contrast, learning incorporates all education but it is something much broader and often far less planned.

Demographic factors play an important role in the development of lifelong learning. It is a truism that people are living longer, but it is also significant that it is being recognized that older people are still capable of enjoying the fruits of learning. For instance, recent research in psychology, developing the ideas of fluid and crystallized intelligence from Cattell's (1943) early work, demonstrates how individuals continue to develop both crystallized and fluid abilities as a result of learning throughout the whole of their lives. Lohman and Scheurman (1992, p 86) for instance, argue that adults:

> continue to develop those abilities that they use; abilities that show decline in the later adult years either emphasize speed or require the solution of novel problems. In both cases, disuse may be a significant factor in explaining the decline.

In other words, the more people continue to have experiences and learn from them, the more their abilities grow and develop; only when they choose not to be involved in the experiences of everyday living do they cease to learn, grow and develop. As Senge (1990, p 142) suggests, learning is about 'expanding the ability to produce the results we truly want in life'. Lifelong learning is more than work life learning, but it may truly be life long.

Lifelong learning as a concept has, however, been hijacked by government reports about the need to continue learning so that individuals might play their part in the knowledge economy. While this is true, it is not exclusively so; but we can see the way in which this is occurring. For instance, in the introduction to the OECD report (1996, p 13), the following appeared:

> Success in realising lifelong learning – from early childhood education to active learning retirement – will be an important factor in promoting employment, economic development, democracy and social cohesion in the years ahead.

In the European Union White Paper (1995, p 18), a similar claim was made:

> The crucial problem of employment in a permanently changing economy compels the education and training system to change. The design of appropriate education and training strategies to address work and employment issues is, therefore, a crucial preoccupation.

In the European perspectives (Collomb and Seidal, in Otala, 1998, p 8), we read the following:

> For Europe to be competitive, working adults need Lifelong Learning: a continual replenishment of their education. Adult Education and Lifelong Learning are essential ingredients in today's integrated Europe.

Even in the rather more utopian Delors Report (1996, p 70) we see that the significance of the economic institution in society is recognized: 'Under the pressure of technological progress and modernization, the demand of education for economic purposes has been constantly on the rise in most countries.'

Moreover, learning is being promoted as something that is good and will automatically bring success to the learners in the knowledge society. Sir Christopher Ball, who initiated the 'Campaign for Learning' in the UK claims:

> Learning pays. Training (at its best) will make nations and their citizens wealthier, societies more effective and content, individuals freer and more able to determine their lives in the way they choose. (Ball, 1992, cited in Longworth and Davies, 1996, p 9)

It is as if the global capitalism underlying this statement is universally good and will produce that good society for which everybody longs. If this discourse is further deconstructed, almost every element is imprecise and might be either wrong or only partly true:

- Learning, which is totally undefined here, in itself does not pay – but learning that is accredited or recognized because it carries a degree or is recorded in a portfolio might help gain a better job. Learning might also help companies produce new products that might be marketable, and so on.
- Training (at its best) will make nations and their citizens wealthier – but unless the commodities are developed and sold, unless there is a market, unless others can afford to purchase those commodities, etc, nobody gets

wealthier, so that at its best, some forms of learning might be a contributory factor in the process.

- Societies might become less effective if people are so learned and articulate that they want to question government and management on every decision and action, or because they recognize that there is much more to life than work.
- Individuals might actually learn that they are not free and are not as able to determine their lives because there are other forces operating, and so on.

Discourse is neither about truth nor falsehood; it is about seeking people to accept the discourse. There is a general tendency to accept what is being proclaimed. Humankind has a will to truth, as it were; we want to know the truth and to believe the discourse. Sheridan (1980, p 128), commenting on Foucault's *Discourse on Language,* wrote this:

> It is as if our culture's apparent veneration of discourse conceals a profound fear of it, as if all the prohibitions and limitations placed upon it were intended to master a threat. If we are to understand the fear, says Foucault, we have a threefold task: we have to question our will to truth, restore to discourse its character as event, and abolish the sovereignty of the signifier.

In other words, we have to recognize that we want to believe it and that we give power to those who frame the discourse, rather than merely regard it as a happening. At the same time, those who continue to frame discourses inaccurately destroy the will to believe it to be truthful, as we are beginning to see as political discourse is being increasing described as 'spin'. But we also need to believe that we must keep on learning so that we will help generate a better standard of living for all and retain our own jobs in the process; within the confines of the system within which we live we may well have to believe it.

This is one of those discourses that we might want to believe because it offers a future that sounds more idealistic and it might well explain for us some of the events that are occurring in our society, and when government, senior management or establishment figures make the claim they might be seen as having the authority to do so. But it is part of the discourse – it is just a tool used by those in power to support and control the present situation. Workers do need to keep on learning, so that we can have a flexible workforce able to respond to the demands of their managers in order that their company can compete in the global market.

Universities have been forced to respond to the demands of the global substructure. Many postgraduate degrees and certificates for vocations have been developed and, as we shall see below, there have been many innovations in teaching to respond to these pressures. Slowly, universities are embracing the idea of lifelong learning, but it is perhaps significant that they were not able to respond in the same way to the demands of older people for non-vocational subjects. Universities of the third age have sprung up all over the UK, unconnected to the higher education system, whereas throughout Europe they are more closely related to the established universities. Universities have traditionally seen their students as being 18- to 25-year-olds and education as occurring in the first periods of life, whereas learning is a lifelong process. The universities have found it much harder to become institutions of lifelong learning. Although funding restrictions have forced them respond to the competitive market, the response has been skewed in the direction of the economic which, in turn, has made many academics question the nature of the university (see Aronovitz, 2000).

Since individuals are learning throughout the whole of their lives – both work life and leisure time learning – they are beginning to seek accreditation for this and universities are beginning to respond to it through the accreditation of prior experiential learning (APEL). This is a process of institutionally recognizing private learning (Jarvis, 1996).

Lifelong education and lifelong learning are now becoming fields of study, as well as fields of practice. Educators, from both the adult and the school sectors, have claimed them as a field of study and practice and there are many conferences run by them. Nevertheless, there is a major danger in this becoming the preserve of one department. This is a field of practice and study of all the professional disciplines and it is necessary for interdisciplinary sharing to occur. Recently (1999), the Queensland library service, in Australia, ran a conference on lifelong learning and it attracted participants from across the range of occupations and disciplines.

Innovations in teaching

Underlying the tenets of the modern university has been the notion that it teaches relevant theory, since knowledge is universal and can be applied to every relevant practice situation. The maxim that 'there is nothing as practical as good theory' has dominated the thinking of many academics. But we can now see that this actually applies only to those situations that are unchanging. In this rapidly changing world, many practice situations are no longer unchanging; many practitioners enter new situations all the time and are required to use their expertise, be reflective practitioners (Schon, 1983) and perform their role in an appropriate manner. Their situation is unique and ephemeral (Jarvis, 1999) and the knowledge that they require is practical knowledge. Several new approaches to teaching practical knowledge have emerged.

One of the most well-attested approaches has been the practice placement, when students have traditionally been placed in a professional practice in order to apply the theory that they have learnt in the university (see Schon, 1987). However, the idea of application of theory to practice is misleading, especially in rapidly changing practice situations. Students do not apply theory but use the information they have gained in the lecture theatre to assist them – this information is like a hypothesis that might work in practice. When they return to the university, therefore, new methods of teaching about what they have learnt in practice need to be used, such as helping them to reflect on practice, to criticize established research reports based on their own practical experience, and so on.

A number of other new approaches have also emerged in recent years, two of which will be mentioned briefly here as illustrations of the direction in which these changes must go – problem-based and work-based learning.

Medicine has led the way in problem-based learning (PBL) and other professions have followed (Boud, 1985; Boud and Feletti, 1991; Kwan, 2000). Sinnott and Johnson (1996) propose that the whole of the university should be reinvented into a problem-oriented institution, although it is clearly possible to integrate PBL with some of the more traditional ways of teaching some forms of *knowledge that*. PBL in medicine started at McMaster University in Canada, but Kwan indicates how rapidly it has spread throughout Asia. It might be regarded as a method of facilitating learning starting from a problem, the solution of which cannot be taken for granted. Kwan (2000, p 136) for instance, suggests in medicine that it is 'the use of a curriculum based on learning of principles, guided by clinically oriented problems set in small groups settings'. He goes on to point out that:

> Knowledge in anatomy, physiology, pharmacology, microbiology, biochemistry, community medicine, etc will all come into place as long as they are of significant relevance to achieving the learning objects of a given HCP (health care problem) as defined by the students. (p 137)

It may be clearly seen that this approach enables integrated practical knowledge to be learnt in professional placement settings. Wilkerson and Hundert (1991, p 165), however, found that: 'An important aspect of problem-based learning. . . is that attention is drawn to the faculty members not having all the answers.' Clearly, not having all the answers creates a major fear for academic staff who have never been trained to teach without having most of the necessary content knowledge to get them through their teaching session. However, the emphasis has now to be placed on the practical knowledge of teaching and on their facilitating learning.

Work-based learning is another new approach, recognizing that workers actually do learn in the workplace. Now the workplace rather than the lecture theatre is the site for the learning for which they are accredited. The key to this approach lies in understanding experiential learning and realizing that practical knowledge is learning during the performance of work roles. The mentor might be someone who, as a senior colleague, acts as a teacher while working with the learner. Several professions have mentors (although they are often called by a variety of other titles) and they provide training for them. Additionally, the learning that occurs in these situations is emotional as well as cognitive: we all bring our emotions, as well as our beliefs and values, to our work situation (see Short and Jarvis, 2000). In these instances, reflective learning, the use of learning diaries and often peer learning groups are fundamental to the process. The worker-learners often meet at weekends so as to have the opportunity to discuss and crystallize their learning experiences.

Once universities start providing opportunities to learn practical knowledge, they are faced with the problem of assessing it. Kwan (2000, p 138) says that McMaster adopted a system of continuous assessment for its PBL course. He says that 'as much attention is paid to the students' learning behaviour and to their understanding of the behavioural and population perspectives as to the biological perspectives of problem-based learning'. There are, however, a number of other approaches that might be used such as reflective journals, reflective essays, specific practical assessments, and even *viva voce* type examinations.

These approaches call for considerable changes in universities' way of assessing this form of knowledge, since they are no longer assessing 'correct' knowledge but the learners' understanding of practice and the rationality of their choice of role performance, and so on. Now what is being assessed is not necessarily correct role performance, although it might be this when organizational procedures prescribe role performance, but also the workers' or learners' reasons for acting in the way that they do. This requires that academics learn new ways of assessing and universities change their traditional procedures quite considerably.

Distance education

At the heart of globalization lies information technology, enabling *knowledge that* to be disseminated around the world. Information technology has re-aligned time and space. Traditional teaching and lecturing have taken place at the time when the knowledge was taught. Writing actually enables all teaching to be learnt at a later time than when it was shared – this is 'time–space distanciation' (Giddens, 1990). With the advent of the printing press, time–space distanciation developed and became a taken-for-granted phenomenon – books enabled people to read authors' thoughts long after they had been written.

The major universities started their own publishing businesses to disseminate information widely but, in retrospect, it is surprising that the universities did not develop distance education systems earlier than they did. With the advent of mass production, it became even easier to prepare distance education material (Peters, 1984). However, it took the establishment of the British Open University to act as a catalyst for change; universities gradually accepted the fact that adults could learn at a distance and by the 1970s there were some signs of change in some universities. This has enabled some of them to assume a global role; some, like the British Open University, have become mega-universities. It is, as it were, that the universities were beginning to tread the same path as other organizations in industrial society.

However, information technology is not only one of the driving forces for change – it has become an important commodity on the global market. With the rapidity of change the Fordist production methods of the Open University, a university only 30 years old, risked becoming outdated and certainly it has been stretched on occasions to keep the production of its courses abreast of rapidly changing knowledge. Now space and time have been compressed (Harvey, 1990) by electronic communications and the global university becomes a real possibility. The e-university has already been proposed in the UK – it already exists in the USA. But the information technology revolution means that the universities are confronted with even greater challenges. They have to respond to the challenges of globalization in the way that they disseminate knowledge.

It is paradoxical in the knowledge society that universities whose main business is knowledge can be threatened by this age, but it is the case; Duderstadt (1999) entitles the opening chapter of a book: 'Can colleges and universities survive in an information age?' He writes:

> It is my belief that the forces driving change in higher education, both those from within and those from without, are far more powerful that most realize. It seems likely that both the pace and the nature of change in higher education, in America and worldwide, will be considerably beyond what can be accommodated by business-as-usual evolution. (1999, pp 17–18)

Here, then, we see that the powerful forces of information technology – and the global competitive market – are forcing changes on the higher education system that are of momentous importance. Indeed, in Singapore, most new university courses are already prepared for online dissemination, and campuses are 'wirelessed', rather like a room with simultaneous translation facilities, with the whole campus being able to pick up computer signals so that there is no need to plug in the laptop before it can transmit its e-mails, and so on. Within a few years all students and staff will have laptops and then even the nature of the campus will change.

The authors of the various chapters in *Dancing With the Devil* (Katz and Associates, 1999) indicate some of the challenges that universities face. They recognize that there are manufacturers of learning materials other than universities and that they are also involved in the competitive global market of selling their knowledge. Universities are, therefore, facing challenges to which they have to respond with alacrity. But, according to Blustain *et al* (Katz and Associates, 1999, pp 70–71) universities are facing tremendous barriers to change, including:

- fixed costs for academic staff;
- fixed costs for physical plant;
- pre-Gutenberg pedagogical methodology;
- professional paradigms that prevent collaboration between academic and technical staff;
- little leverage in professional models, so that the economics of education are controlled by the size of the lecture theatre;
- the large initial investments required in technology;
- the non-business or anti-business orientation ethos in universities.

In addition, the World Wide Web now provides the equivalent of a vast university library, much of it freely available to anybody who logs on and has the expertise to surf it successfully. Yet this massive resource is not unlimited, because some specialist knowledge and much historical knowledge is harder to trace on the Web. Even so, the Web exists and is a resource that universities must learn to use.

The Web is already causing universities problems in other ways, since students can plagiarize material from it and the academic staff may be completely unaware. This is, then, another reason for changing the methods of assessment from seeking to assess 'correct' knowledge to assessing reasoned practical knowledge.

The substructural forces of the global society are driving these changes. There is little or nothing that universities can do to stop them occurring, especially as some of the other providers of knowledge are already involved in the utilization of electronic forms of delivery. Universities do face major threats but this does not signify the end of face-to-face tuition. Some electronic bubbles have already burst on the stock market, suggesting that people are not totally enamoured by impersonal delivery systems, and so there is every reason to be confident that people will come to more traditional teaching and learning sessions – but they might not come on a residential or even a full-time basis. Prime-time learning may occur in summer and weekend schools, etc, as well as part-time teaching blocks of a week or so. Yet even these are expensive and so they have to be carefully planned, value for time and money exercises. Universities find it tremendously difficult to cater for the part-time student who is also a business executive and who may want the same type of business facilities that the ordinary hotel supplies as a matter of course. Hence, even hotels are competitors with the universities for this prime-time face-to-face learning.

Universities are no longer the only organizations whose existence relies on knowledge. Knowledge-intensive corporations are the same. They create and use knowledge. Many other professional practitioners who function in the rapidly changing world also create knowledge by their practice, and so there is a sense in which, by their learning in new practice situations, they are undertaking a form of research.

Learning and research

Contemporary society is a rapidly changing one; practitioners cannot always presume upon their practice situations and so they are sometimes faced with disjuncture. Disjunctural experiences are often ones in which individuals ask why or how. These are the questions that commence the learning process and, unsurprisingly, they are also the questions that commence the research process.

Like learning, research is a process of transforming experience, sometimes through a reasoning process, but often through much more controlled methods and techniques of seeking information. It is proactive. Indeed, it is a process of learning – it is a form of learning, but it does not incorporate all learning. Research is a restricted form of learning employing rigorous methods of discovering and analysing data.

It is not surprising that professional practitioners, working in rapidly changing environments, are not just seeing their place of work as a site for learning; they are now seeing it as a place for research. Practitioner researchers have emerged at this time because practice is changing rapidly, and we can no longer assume that research conducted in the past is replicable in the future. In addition, as practical knowledge is now relative and changing rapidly, it is essential for knowledge-based workers to keep abreast of these changes and to continue their education.

Research has traditionally been associated with the empirical and the scientific – something that has high status knowledge, so that researchers were automatically treated as people from the upper echelons of the learned society. Indeed, this high status is reflected in the fact that, as McNiff (1988, p 13) has rightly claimed, 'The epistemology of the empiricist tradition is that theory determines practice. Teachers are encouraged to fit their practice into a stated theory.' We have shown that this approach is false, but this has downgraded the status of those who generate this knowledge to which everybody had to conform. Research is something that practitioners can and should undertake; the generation and control of knowledge and its associated high status have been undermined. Neither research nor the researchers can now be distanced from everyday practice and ordinary practitioners as they were in the past. Indeed, practitioner researchers (Jarvis, 1999) have broken down these boundaries and research has been democratized. But this means that instead of the occasional PhD student in a department, there might be a hundred – many part-time and undertaking their own research based on their practice. This has added to the workload of academics, but it has both changed the nature of supervision and also the way that research is viewed. Perhaps some universities are going to be forced to concentrate on teaching and researching beyond the first degree. The boundaries of society have become more open; more people can penetrate the apparent mysteries of 'scientific' research and research itself has become much more part of everyday practice. Lyotard (1984, p 48) makes a similar point about education as a whole:

> The transmission of knowledge is no longer designed to train an elite capable of guiding a nation towards its emancipation, but to supply a system of players capable of acceptably fulfilling their roles at the pragmatic posts required by its institutions.

Research, overall, is now about helping the system, organization or practice to improve its performance – which is precisely what action research has claimed. Research then is no longer only a function of the elite, by the elite, for the elite. Practitioner research is now part of the knowledge research, which itself has become a more democratic phenomenon, the outcomes of which can be more broadly used in society.

It is perhaps natural that in societies using rapidly changing knowledge, learning and research should be seen to be closely related and that this form of research might be seen as part of a learning society.

Conclusion

In this chapter we have begun to relate knowledge and learning and have seen how the teaching role of university academics has changed as the nature of knowledge has changed. We have looked at the nature of learning and we have seen how experiential learning means that practitioners are generating their own practical knowledge in the workplace and, consequently, they are becoming practitioner researchers. This is calling for major changes in universities and so we now turn to the relationship between universities and the learning society.

5

Universities and the learning society

Knowledge and its dissemination have always been the business of the universities, but in the previous two chapters we have seen how the neo-liberal forces of global capitalism have created massive changes in society's knowledge that have forced the universities to re-examine their own mission. The outcome of our argument in the previous chapters has been that since knowledge can no longer be regarded simply as 'truth', the place of didacticism is being questioned and learning has now become the focus of attention. It is no accident that many documents now refer to the 'learning society', the 'learning city', the 'learning organization' and so on. The Dearing Report (1997) for instance, specifies that it is looking at the place of higher education in the learning society. In this chapter we will examine the universities in the learning society, and we will also look at learning cities and learning organizations. By way of conclusion, we will point to the universities themselves as learning organizations.

The learning society

The learning society is both a confused and a confusing idea. Indeed, one of the phenomena that makes society a society is a sense of permanence and patterns of behaviour. In other words, members of society repeat certain fundamental processes, like language and behaviour patterns and so non-learning is a feature of society (Jarvis, 1987). If learning either produces change or reflects it, then the nature of society is itself changing. This we know to be the case, since change is endemic. But not everything is changing; there is still a degree of stability and permanence. There is both learning and non-learning.

Coffield (2000, p 28) actually suggests that all talk of *'the* learning society will have to be abandoned rather than refined' (emphasis in the original); he says that there are simply too many modern and postmodern readings of the term for any general agreement on one approach or model to be possible. He highlights 10 different approaches from the various research projects on which he reports (p 8):

1. skills growth;
2. personal development;
3. social learning;
4. a learning market;
5. local learning societies;
6. social control;
7. self-evaluation;
8. centrality of learning;
9. a reformed system of education;
10. structural change.

A number of things emerge from these 10 models. First, they are not different models of a learning society but merely different aspects of the society being studied. Second, they may therefore be describing something of the fragmentation of contemporary postmodern society. Third, they have neither a sophisticated nor an agreed model of learning on which to base the analysis, which prevents genuine comparison of the 14 projects that he reports. Since all the projects were conducted in the UK, I want to argue that it is still possible to talk about a learning society with each of these projects concentrating on but one aspect of the whole. Indeed, these models are actually Western cultural models and societies such as Hong Kong, which is very committed to the creation of a learning society and in which a tremendously high proportion of the adult population attend post-secondary education, provide other perspectives on the learning society.

However, the lack of an agreed definition of learning, which fudges all the political documents on the subject, is a more serious problem – although it is recognized that umbrella terms are necessary in order to include as much of the fragmented society as possible, and 'learning' has become one of these useful but ambiguous terms. Indeed, we have discussed this thoroughly in the previous chapter and we noted clearly that learning is an individual phenomenon: societies and organizations might change but they do not learn. If learning societies are no more than societies that change as a result of social conditions, it both falls into the behaviourist error about learning discussed in the previous chapter – that learning is no more than change and a learning society no more than a changing society – and becomes a virtually meaningless phrase. But it is not true on either count, so we need to explore the relationship between learning and society a little further. It is individuals who learn, but they are social beings. When people learn they sometimes subsequently change their behaviour and/or the procedures of the organization in which they function. This can generate change and the changes introduced into the system might cause other members of the society to learn and change their behaviour or, alternatively, to change their behaviour and learn. But it is the people who learn. The 'learning' might describe a type of society or organization whose structures are designed to cause or encourage people to learn, and it is only in this sense that we can understand the term 'learning society'.

Moreover, we have already pointed out that the substructural forces of globalization are so powerful that they are generating changes in the superstructure all the time. We have suggested that people acquire certain forms of everyday knowledge simply by living in these changing technological conditions, and being forced to keep on changing by the social conditions under which they live. However, this is less true of those who are socially excluded, people in third world countries and so forth, since they are less exposed to these forces of change than those living in the first world, especially those living in urban situations. Globalization is rather like the ripples that appear on the surface of a pond after a pebble has been thrown in. In this case the process starts from three nodal centres, primarily the USA, then Europe and the Pacific Rim. The effects of globalization have spread throughout the world, with the periphery being least affected and consequently excluded from many of the considerations, or when it has been affected it is usually by having the centre's solutions, or policies, imposed upon it – as we saw, for instance, with knowledge management and the World Bank. In this sense, therefore, the learning society is one that is being forced to change and its members to learn.

We can now return to Coffield's 10 types of learning society and see that even within a single society, the forces of change do not produce standardized responses, and nor should we expect this to happen since we have not postulated a deterministic model of society. Nevertheless, we can see that it is possible to classify his types into a smaller number of categories:

- *personal development* – personal development, self-evaluation, centrality of learning;
- *utopian* – social learning, structural change;

- *planned development* – social control, skills growth, reformed system of education, local learning societies;
- *market* – learning market.

It seems from the above that it is possible to argue that those aspects of the learning society that fall under personal development are the natural outcomes of learning. They are about the individual rather than the social, so that we do not need a learning society concept to understand them, although they will have some social outcomes. Nevertheless, when personal development issues involve planning and the control of that development, then they fall into the category of planned development – or strategy. The other three are about vision, strategy and market, and they are distinctly different from each other.

However, one aspect of a learning society not touched upon in Coffield's report is that of learning in the risk society (Beck, 1992) – what Beck calls 'reflexive modernity'. Coffield (2000, p 22) makes an implicit reference to this in his support of Eraut's (1997) definition, discussed in Chapter 4, by saying that his definition takes us beyond 'the anodyne phrase "We're all learning all the time"'. The fact that we are being forced to learn all the time might actually be the very basis of the learning society, which is the outcome of the forces of globalization that are creating change and thereby generating a culture of learning. As we can see, we are all acquiring everyday knowledge that is being changed by the prevalence of scientific and technological knowledge that permeates the cultures of many societies in the world. Only those who have disengaged from society are not really being forced to learn a great deal, and even they are still exposed to some of the forces of change. Much of this is either unplanned or uncontrolled, or both, but it is an aspect that is central to contemporary society – for the learning society is also reflexive modernity (Jarvis, 2000). We see this form of learning as a crucial dimension of the learning society.

We suggest, therefore, that there are four dimensions to a learning society, which we will examine in relation to higher education: vision, planning, reflexivity and market.

Vision

Early writers about the learning society, Hutchins (1968, p 133) for instance, started with an educational vision that everybody would have access to part-time adult education throughout the whole of their lives, but it would also be a society which had 'succeeded in transforming its values in such a way that learning, fulfilment, becoming human, had become its aims and that all its institutions would be directed to this end'. For him, the learning society would be the fulfilment of Athens, made possible not by slavery but by modern machinery.

It was the realization of the computer revolution that led Husen to very similar conclusions. He argued (1974, p 238) that *educated ability* will be democracy's replacement for passed-on social prerogatives'. He recognized that the knowledge explosion would be fostered by a combination of computers and reprographics and he foresaw the possibility of *equal opportunities* for all to receive as much education as they are thought capable of absorbing' (p 240). Despite Sweden's long history of adult education, Husen still regarded the learning society as being educational and based on an extension of the school system.

In a recent book on the learning society, Ranson (1994, p 106) has suggested a similar picture:

> There is the need for the creation of the learning society as a constitutive condition of a new moral and political order. It is only when the values and processes of learning are placed at the centre of polity that the conditions can be established for all individuals to develop their capacities, and that institutions can respond openly and imaginatively to a period of change.

Barnett (1997, p 160) adopts a similar idealistic position when he suggests that a learning society is necessarily a critical society, since he recognizes that there are alternative ways of knowing and yet these need to co-exist in society. Unfortunately, alternatives often lead to power conflicts – the antithesis of Barnett's hopes. Young also adopts an idealistic view, which Coffield (2000, p 24) cites: 'a learning society should embody an education-led economy rather than an economy-led education system', which is something that the neo-liberals would dispute. Indeed, such a claim would assume that education had become the dominant substructural force in society and this appears to be contrary to all the evidence – a vision but one far removed from reality.

The vision of these authors and others who have written on this topic is of a 'good society' that is both democratic and egalitarian; one in which individuals can fulfil their own potential through education and learning. In the UK, the Dearing Report (1997, pp 8–9) also had a section entitled 'A vision for 20 years: the learning society' in which it spelt out the place of higher education in the creation of a learning society. The vision was a balanced one and recognized that the traditional boundaries between vocational and academic education were breaking down and that increasingly active partnerships were emerging. It also recognized, however, that during that period higher education faced considerable challenge as well as opportunities. These would come:

> With increasing competition from developed and developing nations, and given the possibility of locating business operations elsewhere in the world as a result of the development of communications and information technology, nations will need, through investment in people, to equip themselves to compete at the leading edge of economic activity. In the future, competitive advantage for advanced economies will lie in the quality, effectiveness and relevance of their provision of education and training, and the extent of their shared commitment to learning for life. (Dearing, 1997, p 13, para 24)

The Dearing report recognizes that universities are facing considerable challenge and that the vision is one that is fundamentally vocational. The year after Dearing reported, there was a UNESCO world conference on higher education in Paris and this conference also had a vision for the universities. The report claimed:

> The traditional missions of higher education systems (to educate, undertake research and provide services to the community) are still valid, but we affirm that their main mission nowadays is to educate responsible citizens, providing an open space for higher education and for learning through life. (UNESCO, 1998, para 2)

This report certainly suggests a vision of a good society and sees higher education as an instrument in its implementation. However, the picture that is emerging in this study is that, despite this vision, the universities are being driven by the forces of globalization and are conforming to their demands rather than playing an independent, or even their traditional role in the creation of a democratic society. Aronovitz (2000, p 11) writes:

> Far from the image of ivory tower where, monk-like, scholars ponder the stars and other distant things, the universities tend to mirror the rest of society. Some have become big businesses, employing thousands and collecting millions in tuition fees, receiving grants from government and private sources, and a selective few raising billions in endowments.

While his picture might depict many universities in the USA, the response to these demands has not been uniform throughout the world, so that it might be false to say that the substructure is *determining* the shape of the university for the future. There still is a vision, but how does it fit into the plans for the learning society?

Planning

There have been many policy documents published by European governments in recent years, all illustrating the strategies that they regard as important in the development of the learning society. It is unnecessary to make reference to many of these here, but they also recognize the significance of the knowledge economy.

In the introduction to the OECD report (1996, p 13), the following appears:

> Success in realizing lifelong learning – from early childhood education to active learning retirement – will be an important factor in promoting employment, economic development, democracy and social cohesion in the years ahead.

In the European Union White Paper (1995, p 18), a similar claim is made:

> The crucial problem of employment in a permanently changing economy compels the education and training system to change. The design of appropriate education and training strategies to address work and employment issues is, therefore, a crucial preoccupation.

In the British government report *The Learning Age* (DfEE, 1998a, p 13) it is clearly stated that the learning society is something to be created and that it will be educative in nature:

> In the Learning Age we will need a workforce with imagination and confidence, and the skills required will be diverse: teachers and trainers to help us acquire these skills. All of these occupations... demand different types of knowledge and understanding and the skills to apply them. That is what we mean by skills, and it is through learning – with the help of those who teach us – that we acquire them.

Despite the inclusion of some rhetoric about learning enriching our humanity and even our spirituality and the democratic society, the main emphasis of planning in all of these documents is that its end result will be the learner's employability. Dearing (1997, para 28) makes the point quite clearly that:

'We do not see any particular target figure for 20 years time. Informed students and employer demand should be the main determinants of the level of participation in the future.'

Since we know that the main reason why people return to education is work related (Beinart and Smith, 1997) we can once again see that the pressures on the universities to produce occupationally relevant courses are maintained. Indeed, it can be argued that employability is the key to citizenship in contemporary society (Jarvis, 2001b). In addition we have seen that the plans that get reported about what universities are envisaging tend to be vocationally orientated, such as Universitas 21 planning an MBA online (Goddard, 2000b). Universities' planning is, as we might say now, naturally about the way that they can develop courses for which there is a demand, and these tend to be vocational in nature. Their knowledge-base is either 'artificial' or practical and many of them are postgraduate, although it is clear that Dearing (1997, para 28) was recommending that much of this growth should be at a sub-degree level – something that the new foundation degrees in the UK are designed to be and which relates to the work of the corporate universities, as we shall see later in this book.

Reflexivity

The risk society (Beck, 1992) is one in which the complexities of the contemporary world make decisions based on certainty impossible, and uncertainty is introduced into an instrumentally rational world. There are now hardly any points of decision in individual or social life that do not offer alternative viable solutions, and there are rarely any such incidents that have only one certain unequivocal answer. Every decision is a risk, which Beck (1994, p 6) sees as underlying reflexivity:

> Let us call the autonomous, undesired and unseen, transition from industrial to risk society *reflexivity* (to differentiate it from and contrast it with reflection). Then 'reflexive modernization' means self-confrontation with the effects of risk society that cannot be dealt with and assimilated in the system of industrial society – as measured by the latter's institutionalized standards. The fact that this very constellation may later, in a second stage, in turn become the object of (public, political and scientific) reflection must not obscure the unreflected, quasi-autonomous mechanism of the transition: it is precisely abstraction which produces and gives reality to risk society. (Emphasis in the original.)

That society has emerged in the way that it has means that it takes risks when it implements 'solutions' to its problems because there is no necessarily proven answer. Consequently, there is always a need for it to confront itself about the outcomes of the decisions it makes, or fails to make. This is a reflexive society, one of the outcomes of which has been that people are forced to make decisions for themselves, often without having more than the everyday technical knowledge that we discussed in Chapter 3 to guide them. Individuals are forced to take risks, to learn and reflect upon their decisions, and so forth. They are also forced to adjust to the changes that occur in society as a result of whatever changes occur. As Beck (1994, p 13) suggests, individuals 'must produce, stage and cobble together their biographies themselves'. People must decide for themselves, adjust to social changes and keep on learning, either by doing and reflecting upon the outcomes, or thinking and planning before the action takes place. In another sense, creative discoveries and new decisions made in the workplace are also individual learning. As Beck (1994, p 16) claims, participation in work in reflexive societies 'in turn presupposes participation in education' – or at least in learning. One of the outcomes of reflexive modernization is that individuals are learning more often throughout the whole of their lives – both reflectively and non-reflectively. This is 'learning all the time' but it is not an anodyne statement, rather a necessary feature of reflexive modernity. In this sense a reflexive modern society must be a learning society, but the learning is individual and much of it is autonomous and occurs outside of the institutionalized provision of learning opportunities.

There are at least two aspects to this element of the learning society that impinge on universities. The first is that a great deal of scientific and technological knowledge is being generated or rejected as they seek to discover whether or not the policies introduced to respond to the problems are correct or successful. University research is clearly involved both in generating some of the scientific knowledge upon which some of the decisions are made – although transnational corporations also make a lot of these decisions based on their own research – and in monitoring the implementation of these decisions in a reflexive mode. Universities are also responding to these changes pedagogically, by introducing new courses at both undergraduate and postgraduate level for the workforce.

As society changes with all the technological innovations, individuals are forced into situations where they either have to learn about specific technologies in order to function normally in contemporary society, or they act in response to new pressures and do something, later realizing that they have actually acquired new knowledge as a result. In both of these situations they acquire everyday technological knowledge. In the history of university extramural education for adults, many programmes have been mounted in order to acquaint people with the new discoveries and new forms of knowledge, although as society becomes even more complex nearly every new technical commodity purchased has instructions about how to use it – unplanned self-directed learning has become a feature of the learning society. People are forced into a learning mode by the very complexity of the commodities that they purchase and it is not uncommon to hear people say how difficult it is to understand the instructions – the writers of these are not trained in the art of writing learning material.

Market

Contemporary society is also a consumer society and the history of consumerism can be traced back to the 18th century. Campbell (1987) traces it back to the romantic period in the 18th century, when pleasure became the crucial means of realizing that ideal truth and beauty which imagination had revealed and, significantly, this romantic movement 'assisted crucially at the birth of modern consumerism' (Campbell, 1987, p 206), so that a longing to enjoy those creations of the mind becomes the basis for consuming new phenomena. In other words, there can be no market economy unless there are consumers who want to purchase the products that are being produced. Advertising plays on imaginary pleasure – and learning becomes fun! While learning was equated with education in people's minds, they remembered their unpleasant experiences at school when it was no fun to learn and a barrier to further education was erected, one that every adult educator sought to overcome.

As we pointed out earlier, one of the advantages of the concept of learning is that it is a consumer term, whereas 'education' is a producer concept. Once learning became separated from education, then learning could become fun – and there is a sense in which this has become a more popular thing to do in the UK since the creation of the British Open University. Now people could learn all the things that they have wanted to learn, and they do not have to go to school to do it. They can read books, watch the television, listen to the radio and go and talk with other people – if they want to. The Open University marketed a commodity, and other organizations have followed suit. Now people can learn by purchasing their own multimedia personal computers and surfing the Web, watching the television learning zone programmes, buying their own 'teach yourself' books and magazines and even their own self-directed learning courses.

Schumpeter (1976) actually argued that one of the strengths of the market is that it has necessarily to be innovative. In order to compete in the global learning market, there has been an expansion of all forms of provision of learning opportunities worldwide – both in what is offered and how it is offered: from traditional face-to-face teaching in a 'real-time' situation to the utilization of a variety of teaching and learning methods in realigned time and space. This expansion is not only made possible by the advance of information technology but also by the globalization of the English language.

Universities in general are now in the educational market, offering learning opportunities at all levels, including research degree programmes, for those who need the education for their work, or for those who just want to enrol in the educational programme for self-fulfilment, fun, or for other reasons. The universities have structured their courses for the market: many are offered by mixed-mode delivery and some entirely by distance learning; they tend to be modular, some more practically orientated, and accreditation is offered for short courses. For instance, awards worth a specified number of credits are offered for very short courses that can be incorporated at a later date into a more major qualification. A Master's degree is now often divided into three postgraduate qualifications: a postgraduate certificate, a postgraduate diploma and a Master's degree. As Baudrillard (1988) has argued, phenomena need symbols in order to become marketable. Learning has become an aspect of symbolic capital (Bourdieu, 1984).

> Knowledge becomes important; knowledge of new goods, their social and cultural value, and how to use them appropriately. This is particularly the case with aspiring groups who adopt a learning mode towards consumption and the cultivation of a lifestyle. It is for groups such as the new middle class, the new working class and the new rich or upper class, that the consumer-culture magazines, newspapers, books, television and radio programmes which stress self-improvement, self-development, personal transformation, how to manage property, relationships and ambition, how to construct a fulfilling lifestyle, are most relevant. Here one may find most frequently the self-conscious auto-didact who is concerned to convey the appropriate and legitimate signals through his/her consumption activities. (Featherstone, 1991, p 19)

Knowledge production has become an industry (a theme to which we shall return in the final chapter of this book), cultivating the desire of people to learn. The learning society has now become a learning market. However, the purpose of entering the market is economic gain. Providers will produce whatever commodity will sell, and while it may help some people self-fulfil, these will only be the individuals who have both the time and the finance to be able to afford to purchase in the marketplace of learning. The market has no morals and so the vision appears to be nothing other than rhetoric for both higher education and the learning society.

However, one significant difference arises between what the university used to be and all institutions that produce knowledge for the market. The universities, as Foucault reminded us, were involved in humankind's will to truth; now they produce knowledge for other purposes, either so that commodities can be produced from the knowledge that has been discovered or as learning materials themselves – both for the market. The largest purchaser of the universities' output is the world of work. Knowledge has now become information packaged and presented for sale, retailed by, among others, the universities.

The learning society is a product of globalization and in the rhetoric at societal level we have seen that universities are still regarded as instruments for creating the better society. However, since neither nation states nor the universities are powerful enough to control the market, they may in their different ways only influence its future global direction but, as we have already pointed out, there are local elements to globalization, and these are manifest in the idea of the learning society as learning towns and cities and learning organizations.

Learning cities

As we pointed out in Chapter 2, universities are part of the social capital of a locality; they have a role to play in their region. The concept of the learning city dates back to the early 1970s, although the first international conference on the topic was held in Barcelona only in 1990, followed by several others. The OECD and the UK have both taken a major role in promulgating the idea. Indeed, in 1993, Whitbread plc sponsored a report, *Teaching and Learning in Cities*, edited by Learmonth (1993). The object of this report was expressed by Thomas Sobol, writing about the USA, in the Introduction:

> But today our schools are under siege. Dramatic changes in the world have rendered much that we do obsolete and imposed upon us new demands. We cannot tolerate any longer a system in which many of our students are inadequately prepared for higher education or the workforce. We cannot tolerate that many of our most academically successful students lag behind their age mates in other industrialized countries in their knowledge of mathematics, sciences, languages, and history.

It might immediately be asked why reference to schooling should be made in a book about universities, and Sobol answers this nicely by quoting an African proverb: 'It takes a whole village to raise a child.' Schools have to learn to work collaboratively with all the organizations and institutions in the community, including the local universities and corporations. Powell (1993), in the same report, cites a project in Cincinnati in which Ohio State University and eight other schools and colleges collaborated with the schools in a variety of different programmes:

- in-service for primary science teachers;
- preparation of teachers in alternative teaching approaches, eg Montessori;
- summer enrichment for children;
- young authors;
- education for minorities;
- encouraging children to take up careers in engineering;
- preparing young people for college.

American universities, unlike their British counterparts, have always regarded community service as an intrinsic part of their work. The responsibility in the UK for many of these activities has been the welfare state, but as welfare provision has declined schoolteachers have been pressurized to undertake a variety of tasks in order to meet the educational needs of the students for whom they are responsible, for which they might need assistance from their local universities. But while there is no specified tradition of service to the community in British universities, many academics do assume many responsibilities in their local communities, for which they get no additional recognition in the universities. Nevertheless Schutte and van der Sijde (2000, p 7) take for granted that service is the third element of the universities' task, and McGivney (1999) reports on a number of community initiatives in the UK where the universities have been involved.

The University of Sussex, for example, has used funding from a number of courses to provide learning activities, educational guidance and support for people living in housing estates outside of the nearby towns of Brighton, Hastings and Crawley. Adults gained educational qualifications at level 1 in higher education and at least 50 were registered for certificates in higher education. In Scotland, another scheme (Scottish Wider Access programme) used higher education staff both to teach and prepare students to cope with the demands of university life. Shattock (2000) specifies how the University of Warwick has had a major impact on the local community. Goddard (1999) illustrates the way in which the University of Newcastle has contributed to the development of the local learning region, and he makes a number of recommendations about the way that universities can continue to contribute to the knowledge economy of the local region. Indeed, the study by Schutte and van der Sijde (2000) on the universities and their regions, which is about the European Consortium of Innovative Universities, concentrates on the economic rather than the cultural impact that these universities are having on their local regions. With few exceptions, such as Warwick, the arts, humanities and issues of local democracy are rarely mentioned. The emphasis is on the wealth production to which universities can contribute, although some of the major problems of the global market, which have been discussed earlier in this book, are omitted. In the next chapter, we will return to this within the context of university provision for staff development of local employing organizations.

Perhaps the UK can learn something from the University of Hong Kong's initiative in lifelong learning and the local community. In 1999, the Education Committee of Hong Kong called for a broad-based and flexible curriculum for post-secondary education necessary to meet the needs of the community. It was decided by the Director of the School of Professional and Continuing Education (SPACE) that, in response to this report, it should open a local community college to provide school leavers with opportunities to study for a Certificate in General Studies (one year), an Advanced Certificate in General Studies (two years) and an Associate Degree (three years). The college would provide student-centred education, offer an educational support and career guidance service, and its qualifications would be recognized for entrance to universities around the world for their full bachelor degree programmes. In September 2000, about six months after taking the initial decision, the college was staffed, opened and had its first 740 enrolments. Since the community college is self-supporting and was initially funded by SPACE, it is possible to see how universities can play a major role in the education of their local region.

The Department for Education and Employment in the UK published a report (DfEE, 1998c) on learning towns and learning cities, in which some 19 towns and cities are mentioned – although this is not a complete list. Towns and cities in other countries, such as Australia, are embarking upon similar schemes. In all of these initiatives, partnerships have been established to pursue the aim of creating in their locality a culture conducive to learning. In a number of them universities have been regarded as active partners in the project and in some, such as Edinburgh, universities have contributed some funding. Local businesses have also played a role in many of these partnerships. However, we found (Jarvis *et al,* 1997) in a research project conducted in the City of London that where businesses have their own programmes of learning for their staff, they were unwilling to support learning initiatives that might distract them into other forms of learning.

The learning city initiative is one that can be relevant to towns, villages and hamlets. While it is not entirely devoted to preparing people for the workforce, nor should it be, it is one in which universities might be involved with their region. Nevertheless, the need for people to be educated in order to be employable is not far from the surface in all of these schemes.

The learning organization

Traditionally, it has been taken for granted that the most efficient way to organize people was through a system of legally or rationally accepted rules or procedures, with power residing in the appointed office-holder at different levels in the hierarchy (Weber, 1947, pp 329–41). The assumption underlying this was that society was static and the rules and regulations would be relevant for a considerable period of time. When change was necessary, it could be introduced by the relevant office-holder at the appropriate level, and those beneath that level would merely accept it and conform. But what we are now seeing is that there are dramatic changes in society, and organizations have to respond more rapidly to change than bureaucratic procedures allow. Power still resides in office in many organizations but those that are responding rapidly to the changing social pressures accept the fact that knowledge is power, irrespective of the position of the knowledge-holder in the organization. Those who know become the teachers of others who learn. The organization responds by accepting the authority of knowledge and the knowledge-holders become leaders in the organization irrespective of office. Everybody in the organization who has knowledge useful or relevant to the organization has regular opportunity to feed it back into the system and influence the way that it functions. The learning organization is, in this sense, the antithesis of bureaucracy.

Swieringa and Wierdsma (1992, p 33) describe the learning organization in terms of organizational learning:

> we mean the changing of organizational behaviour. The changing of organizational behaviour is a collective learning process – an organization has not automatically learnt when individuals within it have learnt something. Individual learning is a necessary but not sufficient condition for organizational learning.

In other words, procedures need to change and the organization has to grow more responsive to the demands made upon it.

Many corporations have been experimenting with approaches to the learning organization for a number of years. Watkins and Marsick (1993, p 8) suggest that these organizations share the same features:

- leaders who model calculated risk taking and experimentation;
- decentralized decision making and employee empowerment;
- skill inventories and audits of learning capacity;
- systems for sharing learning and using it in their business;
- rewards and structures for employee initiative;
- consideration of long-term consequences and impact on the work of others;
- frequent use of cross-functional work teams;
- opportunities to learn from experience on a daily basis;
- a culture of feedback and disclosure.

Universities are organizations and they should be learning organizations. It is, therefore, useful to look at the features of the learning organization suggested by Watkins and Marsick (1993) above. We shall return to these in the following chapter, but few seem to reflect the current university culture, and so we might ask ourselves whether universities whose business is knowledge are actually able to become learning organizations, or learning universities. Duke (1992) addressed this question, as we shall see below.

Senge (1990, pp 18–25) asks whether an organization has a learning disability, and he suggests seven major ones:

1. I am my position – the role holder's pride of position.
2. The enemy is out there – but we are all right.
3. The illusion of taking charge – the senior managers are in control.
4. The fixation on events – rather that looking at systems as a whole.
5. Working too fast and not being able to see what is happening beyond the organization.
6. The delusion of learning from experience – the longer people are in a position, the more unlikely they are to be able to solve its problems by innovative solutions.
7. The myth of the management team – but most organizations have them.

It should be noted that Watkins and Marsick and Senge are not necessarily in disagreement about learning from experience. The delusion about which Senge writes refers to the form of learning from experience that results in habitualization and confidence so that the office holders think that they know the answers to the problems. In contrast, Watkins and Marsick claim that people need to learn from experience every day rather than rest content in their experience, so that habitualization does not occur.

It could be claimed that this book is about 'the enemy out there', and in one sense it is – but it is more than that. Globalization is something that is happening and with which universities might not be entirely happy, and it might be an enemy to the university and the development of scholarship – but it should not be an excuse for inertia, nor is it the whole reason for universities' crises. Senge's list of disabilities might reflect some departments and some universities and some of the reasons for their crises.

Watkins and Marsick (1993, pp 187–91) turn to the issue of globalization and suggest that it has been a transforming force for many companies. For them, however, globalization actually means internationalization rather than the economic globalization upon which this book is based, and far more efficient communication within the whole. Yet the story they tell about Whirlpool Company executives meeting together face-to-face across national and cultural boundaries and working out what the international dimension means to the company has resulted in changes in the way that the company is managed. But they recognize that there is still no mechanism to help understand what prevents people from thinking globally, nor how the company can measure the outcomes of its global thinking conferences. At the same time, the example they provide raises questions about the extent to which the company actually is a learning organization, since their illustration is still a top-down model. Indeed, much of the literature on the learning organization points to the difficulties that individuals have had in introducing change into the system (see also Pedler *et al*, 1996). Indeed, Meister (1998, p 69), citing Schueller of the University of Chicago Hospital Academy, indicates that:

> it is impossible for a highly bureaucratic organization in a regulated industry to move directly to a learning organization. 'It takes years to get there, and there are developmental steps along the way. For us, the corporate university is based upon multiple learning tracks; multiple learning offerings; learning that is targeted for all employees, as opposed to just management or just physicians or just nurses. And it provides career development ladders to move into other positions in the learning organization'.

The corporate university is seen as an important step in creating the learning organization; at the heart of the new British Aerospace Virtual University is a Faculty of Learning, which points to the fact that among the new corporate universities, learning is seen to be the key to growth and development (Kenny-Wallace, 2000).

Perhaps it is appropriate to return to Beck's (1992) position in *The Risk Society* – making decisions and policies without knowing the outcomes is a risky business. Indeed, all learning is paradoxical (Jarvis, 1992) since, in this case, there is both fear and excitement. For some learning is a fearful business and they prefer not to learn – they prefer the status quo. In precisely the same way, we cannot expect everybody within an organization to embrace risk and excitement, and we can expect many to prefer the comfort of the status quo. Motivating people to learn and to change is one of the necessary skills of management and a great deal of change comes slowly. Learning organizations may be able to point to specific incidents where considerable change occurs as a result of learning, but they may also be able to point to many situations where there has been resistance to further learning.

Universities are organizations whose business is knowledge, and so we might expect that universities should stand as good a chance as any organization of being a learning organization.

Conclusion

Before our understanding of globalization had really developed, Knapper and Cropley (1985) examined the way that higher education was adapting to lifelong learning. They clearly recognized the constraints that academic and administrative staff would impose on universities adapting to the demands of lifelong learning. With much insight they wrote:

> Integrating and co-ordinating all forms of post-school education would also raise crucial questions in the area of decision making. Universities, for example, would be reluctant to give up any of their independence, or to sacrifice their right to be the sole arbiters of what is academically worthwhile and what is not. Many university staff members could be expected to be loath to accept new definitions of competence, or to work side by side with practitioners who may have very limited formal qualifications and no research experience. Issues of this kind mean that traditional institutions of higher education would be confronted by problems not only of a straight-forward management kind, but also by issues of status and power. (Knapper and Cropley, 1985, p 80)

They go on to point out some of the practical considerations that would also have had to be taken into account and illustrate how difficult it was, and still might be, for universities to become learning universities. In 1992, Duke returned to this topic and again he recognized that change in universities is hard to achieve. He reaches the conclusion of his book by pointing to the fact that change occurs through stealth rather than by other means; change has occurred but much of it is hardly recognized because it has happened slowly and was not heralded from the rooftops. In 1999, he and several colleagues (Bourgeois *et al*, 1999) were still forced to conclude that the adult university had not yet really occurred and enrolling more adult students had not really resulted in the ethos of the university changing. They remain optimistic that individuals have the capacity to become actors in making their own and society's future — but whether they will have the type of vision Barnett (1990) had when he asked about the nature of higher education may be another matter.

We now need to examine the extent to which universities need to change, or to resist it. In the UK, they have endeavoured to adopt something of a corporate image and copy the large companies, but how much this has enabled them to become learning universities and respond to contemporary social pressures is much less certain.

6

The corporate university (academy) of the university

Universities, founded by Church and state, have traditionally undertaken research according to the demands of the academic disciplines and taught a wide range of subjects – many of which change much more slowly than do the positive and technical forms of knowledge. They have been funded by their founders, but mostly by the state, so that they have not had to operate in a competitive global market. There is a sense, therefore, in which they reflect post-Enlightenment modernity, rather than the post-1970s late modernity. Since the 1970s, however, they have been exposed to the substructural pressures of global society to change. This process was exacerbated at the beginning of the 1980s in the UK by the neo–liberal monetarist government, decreasing the funding levels of the universities so that they had to become more competitive. This has resulted in many of the traditional universities assuming a more corporate form and functioning more like businesses, with vice-chancellors becoming chief executive officers, collegial governance disappearing, and so on. Brandon (1999, p 126) records how Salford University was forced to do this after the economic cutbacks in the early 1980s and 'to rethink the university role in the context of the needs of the business community'. British universities moved in the direction of corporate reform following recommendations made to them by a committee chaired, ironically, by the chairman of a company that itself has found considerable difficulty in responding to the demands of contemporary society.

In the USA, Aronovitz (2000, p 83) blames the end of the Cold War for universities becoming corporations:

> When the Soviet Union collapsed, research support took a nosedive. Every President or Chancellor of a major university immediately donned CEO clothes and aggressively sought investors from the private sector. By the mid-1990s, the corporate university had become the standard for nearly all private and public schools.

It should be noted that Aronovitz uses the term 'corporate university' in a different manner to the way that it is used in this book. For him, it is the traditional university becoming more like a corporation whereas it is used here for those institutions founded by corporations for their own education and training purposes, but which they call universities. Throughout his study, he documents how the universities have had to behave like corporations, restructuring themselves, downsizing and so on, in order to survive financially, or even to move into profit.

However, corporations are facing the same sets of pressures as the universities, and they are being forced to look seriously at their own organizational structures and performances. Their structures tend to be a little more dynamic than those of the university and in order to compete in the global economy, they have also had to look carefully at the way that they treat and train their own staff – which has included starting their own corporate universities.

This book is not a study of the way that corporations are changing, so we will make only brief reference to this in the opening section of this chapter. In the next section we will examine a proposal that instead of only seeking to copy corporations in respect of their economic activities, universities should copy them in relation to the development of their staff, anticipating in this second section the content of the next chapter. In the final section of this chapter we will examine some of the issues that face the normal universities in the light of the foregoing discussion.

The corporate nature of the university

Three areas of university life will be examined in this section: university administration and structures, the pedagogic offering of the universities and research. Considerable reference has been made to each throughout the previous chapters of this study and some of the references will assume that the previous chapters have been read.

University administration and structures

One of the outcomes of the administrative changes introduced in the 1980s in the UK is that universities were encouraged to become more corporate and managerial in their administration. The power of university senates and faculty boards declined in the face of vice-chancellors becoming chief executive officers with their senior management teams; an ideology that trickled down to the heads of schools and faculty deans, who in turn created their own 'offices' and formed their senior management teams at a lower level.

The idea was to make universities more efficient in this business world. One of the immediate outcomes was to dis-empower many academics who had attended the traditionally important university meetings, such as senate and faculty board, but whose function then became merely to rubber-stamp the decisions of the management. But the question was never really asked whether the model proposed was relevant to knowledge-intensive organizations, like universities, in the contemporary world.

Frenkel *et al* (1999, pp 29–30), who conducted a cross-national study of the organization of work in a knowledge economy, suggest that there are three ideal types of work organization: bureaucratic, entrepreneurial and knowledge-intensive, although it must be recognized that ideal types do not necessarily correspond to any single reality and that universities do differ considerably among themselves. Frenkel *et al* describe each type of organization according to work relations (nature and complexity of work), and to vertical (management control and co-worker relations) and lateral (customer and worker) relations. They describe them thus:

> Regarding vertical relations, the B (bureaucratic) type is characterized by hierarchical domination according to specific rules, while the E (entrepreneurial) type effects control by legally enforceable contracts. The KI (knowledge-intensive). . . is based on normative relationships of reciprocity.
>
> The employment relations associated with these three ideal types reflect their respective rationales. The B type requires dependable, diligent workers whose commitment is secured by offering employment security, reasonable pay and internal progression. By contrast, the focus of the E type is more on securing work output and flexibility in response to changes in demand. Thus, contracts for the E type organizations are fashioned so as to provide incentives to adhere to the contract and pay reflects workers' incentives. Finally, the KI type is based on intrinsic motivation aimed at encouraging creativity and innovation.

Universities are knowledge-intensive organizations but they have their bureaucratic procedures and they are being forced to become more entrepreneurial. Consequently, it may be asked whether the universities' administrative structures are sufficiently flexible to allow these three different types of organization in the university to be performed according to the most satisfactory conditions. Even more, it might be asked whether those who are content to perform their bureaucratic procedures are capable of understanding the scholars and research scientists who find their home in a knowledge-intensive organization. Among the crises noted in the first chapter were the pressures being put on university academics, because their work conditions do not enable them to perform their complex roles appropriately. In the UK one only has to look at the bureaucratic procedures of getting courses accredited, quality assurance and research assessment exercises, during which time academics are forced into bureaucratic roles producing papers and engaged in paper-chasing for excessive periods of time. There appears to be a growing number of academics in middle management in universities who profess to be very dissatisfied with their jobs.

Not all academics feel that they are being forced into managerial positions: some have embraced it with considerable eagerness and satisfaction. Newson (1998) for instance, records how some of her radical student colleagues in the 1960s are now the very academics who, as her academic colleagues today, are seeking to change the universities' ethos and embrace even more commercialism. Increasingly, she says, there are signs of corporate influence in the university affairs in Canada and universities are becoming corporations. She claims that managerialism in universities makes it increasingly possible to redirect universities' activities to serve corporate needs. But this is not the whole story: universities also need to create partnerships with industry and commerce and so business executives are appointed to boards of governors, university councils and committees and so forth, which invariably adds to the commercialism and corporate nature of the universities.

Frenkel *et al* (1999, p 276) comment on the way that the management role will probably change, especially in knowledge-intensive industries:

> The term 'manager' will become less meaningful as leadership assumes increasing importance. Leaders' responsibilities will include greater emphasis on interpreting and conveying corporate and business unit values and norms to knowledge workers and communicating the latter's views to senior management. But leaders will not simply act as go-betweens. They will also be expected to embody the entrepreneurial spirit by seeking out and seizing innovative opportunities for their teams to exploit. Leaders will also be responsible for coordinating workers, including selecting and integrating project teams across business units.

In this global knowledge economy, universities need leaders with vision rather than managers who know the correct procedures, and leadership training rather than management training might be a better investment for their long-term future. At the same time, universities also need the administrative structures to enable them to perform not only their knowledge-intensive roles, but also their bureaucratic ones and, increasingly, their entrepreneurial ones.

Pedagogic activities

A mass higher education system is being created in the UK, similar to that which has been operating in the USA for a considerable period of time. But the number of academics employed to teach the increased number of students has barely expanded. Classes are getting larger, standards are harder to maintain and it takes longer to produce the paperwork to prove to quality assurance personnel that the quality remains as high as ever (if it does). Governments, even those claiming socialist origins, have embraced the philosophy of capitalism in forcing university senior management to exploit their workforces in order to produce their commodities at competitive prices.

Undergraduate education is becoming part of initial education, thereby creating a crisis in the higher education system (Lucas, 1996, p 63). Transnational and smaller knowledge-based companies need highly trained staff, even at starting level, and the more they can force governments to undertake the initial training for them, the more likely it is that they will invest in that country. At the same time, there is, as there should be, resistance to the ideology that education is only about vocation – education is for life and not just for work life (see Barnett, 1990).

But it is not only the sheer weight of numbers; it is all the other changes that we have discussed earlier that have resulted in many academics just being able to meet everyday demands by doing all the extra unpaid hours of overtime, to which we referred in the opening chapter. Changes are occurring in teaching, disseminating knowledge and in all other aspects of university work.

It is not just the undergraduate work that has changed. Once these young people have graduated and entered employment, their education must continue so that they can keep abreast of all the innovations being created by advanced technology and with rapidly changing knowledge. Universities have, therefore, begun to adapt to the demands for continuing professional education for these workers. There are more facilities to study part-time for higher degrees, many of which are work-based. For instance, Campbell (1984) records that since 1974 there have been more adults in universities in Canada than traditional-aged undergraduates. This is true of most North American and UK universities. In the UK, for instance, the Higher Education Funding Council reported that in 1993 there were many more people studying in universities who were over the age of 21 than there were traditional undergraduate students. Many of these are professionals (knowledge and service workers) studying for undergraduate and postgraduate degrees part-time, and even at a distance. New postgraduate courses are springing up for different knowledge-based industries – from management to consultancy, from medicine to journalism, and nearly all of them are relevant to the workplace. They tend to place a great deal more emphasis on having a work-based learning format, they are modular in structure and can be studied part-time and/or at a distance – including through electronic modes of delivery.

All these changes take more academic time than the traditional role of the university lecturer. Universities in the West are being forced to change, respond to the market and attract more fee-paying students. If necessary, students have to be offered enticements to enrol, so that the accreditation of prior experiential learning is in danger of becoming the discount price that universities offer to potential students.

This expansion of higher education into lifelong learning is not just a trend for taught courses, it also occurs in student research. An increasing number of individuals researching for PhDs are part-time; their research is work-based and they are often funded by their employers since their research work is either based on the needs of their company or their profession. Universities are also responding to the changes in knowledge and to the pressures of the market and introducing new forms of degrees: practitioner doctorates where there is both teaching of advanced subjects – often work or research-based – and supervising practitioner research.

As global capitalism and the knowledge society have emerged, universities are more exposed to some of these pressures than most other institutions. They are being forced to change: education itself, and especially higher education, is being forced to respond to these substructural pressures. Universities have a more traditional culture and have offered a wider range of subjects than those that are demanded by the global infrastructure, so they may not always be focused on, or be able to respond to market demands sufficiently quickly. This is a point stressed by Niebuhr (1984) who called for a revitalization of America's learning in which he regarded industry and commerce as the agents of change. But the question remains as to whether these market conditions actually provide a revitalization of learning or a restriction on the breadth of learning opportunities open to people to pursue.

Research

Research is perhaps the aspect of the universities' work that is most exposed to the knowledge economy but, curiously enough, not included in the corporate universities' work, as we will show in the next chapter. A great deal of university research in the past has been pursued either because of the academic discipline's demands or because of the research interest of academic staff. But 'blue skies' research can be a costly exercise in which there have been few financial returns. Consequently, the universities are now developing their more recent discoveries and endeavouring to 'bring them to the market'. Among the most successful in doing this has been Stanford University in California; Mercer (1998) estimates that it has produced approximately 1,000 small technology companies and 88 large ones, having more than 100 employees. It is estimated that it has contributed about $31 billion in revenue to the local economy.

Naturally, one of the ways in which a global university can make significant contributions to the good of its region is through its development of knowledge discovered from its own research projects, since it could rightly be argued that if the universities were not involved with these developments, other companies would exploit them for their own ends. Problems emerge, however, when the corporations try to control university research by their grants, endowments of research professorships and so forth. The more that universities come to rely on these grants, the harder it is 'to bite the hand that feeds them'. We referred to the concern expressed by medical researchers in an earlier chapter, and scientists in universities have expressed similar concerns. In *Philanthropy News Digest* (1999), cited earlier, the physicist Irving Lersch is quoted as saying that: 'The commercialization of science has led to a new regime of secrecy that is a great concern to the scientific community. . . secrecy of an entirely new scope and scale.'

While many academics may be expressing concern about the commercialization of research they are also aware that they may have to seek funding for their own research projects from the corporate world. Indeed, their own career promotion might depend on it and, as we have seen in the UK in recent years, their own job security might depend on them remaining silent when their research suggests findings that are contrary to commercial interest or government policy.

The global market is forcing change in many ways in the funding of some universities' research and unless the state provides more funding through its research councils, the universities will have to rely increasingly on corporate funding. Such funding can be beneficent but, as we have already pointed out, it can encroach on traditional academic freedoms. Academics may be forced to accept conditions they do not like simply because they need the grant in order to build up their department's research profile in preparation for the next research assessment exercise. In addition, refusing to accept a grant may make individuals appear disloyal to their universities, which might need the partnership for funding other projects. In this extremely complex world, the pressures on academics to conform to the forces from the economic substructures are growing, making the life of an academic more stressful.

The university's corporate academy (university)

As we have argued throughout this study, universities are becoming more like certain forms of corporation in their structure. There might be nothing wrong with this in itself, provided it enables academic staff to be fully involved in their own academic work, but more research is necessary into the efficiency of university administration systems to demonstrate that this change has actually been beneficial to the universities. It is ironic that in this time of rapid social change we encourage research, but have not always researched our own institutions very thoroughly.

There is another way in which universities might usefully copy the corporations. Universities are increasingly running training courses for their own staff, and in the past they have also frequently encouraged their administrative and support staff to attend local colleges to update their skills. In the UK, until the appraisal system was introduced, however, it was often the staff themselves who had to request permission and financial support to attend courses that were relevant to their updating. Since then, training needs are being more openly discussed in the universities and staff are being provided with more opportunities for continuing their own education. Some universities already organize a regular programme of courses in some administrative areas of their work, including computing. Additionally, universities have introduced courses in teaching and learning, following Dearing's recommendation to create an Institute for Teaching and Learning nationally within the UK. Dearing also suggested that universities should become 'Investors in People' which has a much wider brief that just preparing academic staff to become better teachers, since they should be responsible for the continuing education of all employees.

The need for lifelong learning and human resource development is recognized as being a priority by many corporations. American corporations spend vast sums of money on this. The exact amount of money spent on training in the USA appears to be something of an estimate, but Carnevale *et al* (1990b, p xi) suggested that it was about $210 billion annually a decade ago. Another estimate in 1995 suggested that $52.2 billion (Lucent Technologies, 1996) was spent on corporate universities. Carnevale *et al* (1990a, p 106) also noted that educational institutions provide a great deal of the training and upgrading for the US workforce, although many universities 'have not moved to create special offices that work specifically on customized training programs within industry'. Indeed, it would be fair to claim that they do not have those programmes in place for all their own workforce let alone those of other employers. One beneficial way in which universities could copy the corporates is in creating their own corporate universities or academies – after all, many universities are large employers.

The corporate university is becoming a popular term, the meaning of which is not always clear, since it is used both for traditional universities that have moved in the direction of adopting corporate management structures and a corporate ethos and, more frequently, to describe training programmes in large corporations. The Houston Independent School District (White, 2000) offers a clear and meaningful definition for our purposes. The corporate university is:

> the strategic umbrella for developing and educating employees and its constituents in order to meet the. . . (corporation's). . . purposes. It will be, upon full implementation, the major employee professional development vehicle in the. . . (corporation). It will provide both formal and informal learning opportunities which foster personal and professional growth for individuals in the. . . (corporation) within a respectful, supportive, and positive organizational climate.

The ultimate goal of the corporate university is to create a learning organization. Motorola University claims to be the learning organization of the corporation. It is a system introduced into an organization to provide workplace skills and enhance the corporate culture. Significantly, not all the clients are internal employees; there is a growing emphasis on providing education and training to all the companies in the supply and distribution chains, so that large corporations can spread their influence throughout the whole network within which they operate.

It has been estimated that there will be approaching 2,000 corporate universities at the turn of the millennium and that the annual budgets in 1998 of each one was on average $10.7 million (*Quality Magazine,* 1998). The corporate university need not be in a single or specific place (although some corporate universities do have their own campuses); its mission is to offer education and training to all employees in the companies, and increasingly in their supply and distribution chains. The corporate university is not a university that is adopting a corporate culture as Aronovitz (2000) defines it, but a corporation that is implementing a separate and proactive education and training system.

In the UK, the Dearing Report recognized that universities have to provide training for their academic staff. While the ideas it offered are to be applauded, its conceptualization was based within a traditional university framework with a traditional model of training. But what is suggested here is that universities copy the corporations in their attitude to corporate training. However, it may not only be the supply and distribution chains with whom the universities can work, but also with other partners in the local region, such as the local authorities, health trusts and other agencies. The university employs many staff undertaking similar work to those in other large organizations and if it offers its own staff training and its own qualifications, it could do the same for its partners. Universities need highly trained staff in all of these areas and if they are to become learning universities, then they should require all of their staff to be engaged in continuous learning, and by offering their provision more widely they might not only help themselves but also help their partners to become learning organizations and, incidentally, help fund their own training programmes.

This would mean that universities employ human resource development staff who could assess the work roles of everybody employed within them and establish what training needs they require, if any, to enhance their role performance. In addition, they would need to see how roles could be developed if the role players were to expand their work in response to contemporary demands. Role players could also be prepared for their expanded roles in advance, or at least at the time when they assume them. On visiting a banking training school in Japan about 10 years ago, I was informed by the director that whenever employees changed their job within any of the bank's 300 branches, they were automatically informed when the next course for that job was to be organized and that they were expected to attend.

The universities' programmes could be modular, online or face-to-face and they could be award-bearing – from certificates and diplomas, to foundation and other degrees and even postgraduate awards. In other words, at one end the university's corporate university, or academy, might be offering training that would have traditionally been offered in colleges of further education, and at the other end of the academic range, the corporate university could feed part-time students into the normal university for their courses and practitioner doctorates.

What is being proposed here is that universities should create a corporate university within a university, but that this corporate university should take on a life of its own, while still interfacing with the activities of the normal university. However, it would be unwise to treat it as another department; it needs to be a separate organization working closely with all departments – academic, administrative and support. Its programmes would cater for the needs of the university as a whole and, also, the needs of those organizations with which the university works. Even courses in teaching and learning, or preparing online teaching materials, would be relevant to many of the employees from local organizations, especially in this case schools and colleges. In this way, the university might assume a significant role in the education and training of the workforce in the local region. Some normal universities are already beginning to plan and offer such courses; for instance, City University in London is planning a foundation degree course to be offered to its administrative staff and also to staff from the local authorities and health trusts. However, this initiative remains a one-off rather than part of a larger strategy to produce a corporate university.

The university students are stakeholders in the corporate academy, which might offer additional courses to students in work-related subjects and even relevant to their job applications – from interview techniques to team working and so on. Having educated them and also trained them, as Goddard (1999) notes, they might also play a larger entrepreneurial role in helping locate students in work in their local regions.

It could be argued that this is not the job of the university, but the same might have been said for McDonald's when it started Hamburger University in 1961. In the competitive world of global capitalism and the knowledge economy, corporations have been prepared to go beyond their original brief to train their staff fully in order to become efficient and effective suppliers of the commodities that they supply. One of the signs of this late modern age is that barriers between sectors of society are no longer relevant. In the UK we can bank at Tesco or Sainsbury supermarkets and purchase our electricity supply from the local gas company. Universities, as we know them, are the products of modernity; our structures are not sacrosanct nor are the structures of knowledge, as we have seen in earlier chapters, so universities have to be prepared to adapt their structures in order to play their role effectively. Whether we in normal universities like it or not, knowledge has become a marketable commodity and if we are to supply it efficiently to our students and potential students, we must be prepared to recognize the demands that this makes upon us. In fact, the more efficient universities can become, the greater will be their potential for retaining more of their own academic independence in the global society.

Naturally, there is an alternative to creating a corporate university within the university and that is to outsource all its staff development to an institution outside of the university, such as a local further education college, or a private institution. If the universities did so, the partnership formed could help build even stronger ties between universities and their local colleges, which would also enhance lifelong learning provision in the region.

Universities at the crossroads

Universities are being forced by the pressures of globalization to change and adopt a more corporate ethos; they are powerless to resist this in those countries where the state has adopted a neo-liberal orientation. Consequently, one needs to question the extent to which universities should respond to these social pressures and, if they do so, whether they can change sufficiently fast to respond to the demands of the corporate world for education and training. As 'The university no longer knows what it is to *be* a university' (Barnett, 2000, p 99, emphasis in the original), it is even more difficult for it to decide on how it should respond to the pressures of globalization.

Most universities have already moved steadily in the direction of embracing corporate culture and recognizing that many of their postgraduate students and much of their research will be funded by the corporate world. Professorships are now sponsored by the large companies, research projects funded by them, postgraduate student fees paid by them, and so on. In the world in which we live, it would be surprising if they were not. Moreover, it would be unwise for universities not to be engaged in these enterprises, although they do recognize some of the problems that this produces. Perhaps they need to have an agreed policy at national level in response to them. Universities do need to decide together to what extent they are going to be a partner of, or the 'handmaiden of industry' (Kerr *et al,* 1973). Malcolm Knowles (1991, p 453), one of the USA's leading adult educators for the latter half of the 20th century, wrote about his vision of the university in the 21st century, which did not include the commercial world but did look at the integration of universities into lifelong learning systems:

> My vision scanned across a number of universities. . . I had a hard time finding the universities – they were so well integrated into lifelong learning systems. A few professors were in their studies or laboratories, but most of them seemed to be wandering around among community agencies serving as content resources to learners of all ages, who were carrying out their self-directed learning projects. Some were conducting staff development activities with 'facilitators' employed by those agencies. But a number of them were in the workstation preparing computer-based learning programs, multi-media packages, and other materials for use throughout the learning systems. Few students seemed to be living on campus; the dormitories were operated more like motels, with learners (obviously mostly adults) coming to campus for short workshops. I was impressed by the number of learners who were unquestionably senior citizens.

Knowles' vision for 2016 was described from his own background in adult education rather than other forms of scientific research – but for him, universities would become almost totally integrated into lifelong learning systems. They would lose their distinctiveness.

This, it seems is one of the major questions that face the universities in the global society – are they to become totally integrated into this type of society or are they going to try to retain something that makes the university distinct? We will return to this in the final chapter of this book. Universities need to confront this question. For instance, will they have an agreed policy at a national level:

- about the commercialization of research?
- about the patenting of discoveries in medicine and drugs that will limit provision to those who can afford to purchase them?
- about restricting access to the knowledge reported in research theses, which will change the nature of the university library and the traditional access to knowledge?
- about the traditional freedom of academics to publish the results of their own work, and so on?

Unless there is an agreed national policy between universities, their differences will be exploited by the commercial sector to the detriment of some universities that try to uphold some of the high ideals of the traditional university.

Naturally, there is no agreement between the universities as yet, and some of them are trying very hard to respond to the demands that the corporate world is placing upon them. Much of the university advertising literature is directed at this world. Stanford University, among others, offers a guide to readers of its Web pages about how it collaborates with industry. Governments are also advocating partnerships between normal universities and corporations, since these offer a potential benefit to the national economy. If universities do decide to pursue this path, the question remains as to whether they will be able to change sufficiently rapidly in response to the demands that this world makes upon them.

Eurich (1985, p 15) has suggested that in the USA this has not always been possible:

> Differences in mission between the two systems have led, however, to marked contrast in styles that hamper co-operation. Higher education enjoys a more leisurely and wider time frame. . . To the corporate world, 'time frames' are costly and company controls well understood.

Frequently, starting from opposite poles, co-operation has proved to be neither feasible nor desirable – certainly not mutually satisfactory. It has engendered distrust and discomfort, if not disdain; it has often been abandoned as not worth the effort on either side.

Meister (1998, p 211) echoes these conclusions:

According to a national survey of 1124 adults conducted by the Social and Economic Sciences Research Center of Washington State University, working adults identified busy lives, inflexible course schedules, and the lack of available courses offered nearby as the major barriers to obtaining education and training. What these non-traditional students want is 'just-in-time' education that they can use on the job.

Even so, Eurich went on to point out that there have been many areas of cooperation in the USA, especially with the community colleges – similar to the colleges of further education in the UK.

Her conclusions for the 1980s in the USA might hold good for the UK and other countries at the turn of the millennium. There are many partnerships emerging between them but universities, with few exceptions such as the School of Professional and Continuing Education in Hong Kong which founded a community college in six months, do appear to move much more slowly than does the commercial world. It takes a great deal of time, for instance, to create new courses, new partnerships and new delivery systems. Even those academics having an entrepreneurial understanding have often been frustrated by the bureaucratic procedures of the universities – even those that have adopted a corporate ethos – and so it is hardly surprising that entrepreneurs and companies sometimes look elsewhere for their education and training. Yet it must be understood that from within the framework that universities have adopted, there is often both goodwill and a desire to see change.

Conclusion

In the world of global capitalism, universities have adopted a more corporate approach to their structures, but they have not followed the corporations in the way that they invest in the development of their personnel. It has been suggested here that they should create their own corporate universities, or academies, to provide a more comprehensive education and training system for their own staff and for the employees of their partners.

We have, however, noted the problems that now confront the universities – are they merely superstructural institutions to the global society responding uncritically to its pressures, or is there something that makes the university different? This indecision is one other reason why universities might not be able to respond rapidly to the demands that the corporates make upon them, but in the global marketplace corporates have to act decisively and rapidly. The universities' failure to do so may be one of the reasons why many businesses have started their own corporate universities.

7

The corporate university

The corporate university is, as we saw in the previous chapters and as we have defined it in this study, a strategic umbrella concept for the institutions created for developing and educating employees and the company's constituents in order to meet the corporation's purposes; they are systems of teaching and learning rather than universities in the traditional sense. Additionally, as we will see below and in the final chapter, there are a number of private universities that have been established to sell their educational expertise to industry and commerce, eg Jones International University, which might also be categorized as corporate universities. But then the term 'university' is used about many education and training organizations, such as universities of the third age, people's universities, open universities (not the British Open University), and so on. Naturally, the traditional universities have reacted against this trend, but perhaps there has been something of an overreaction, as Targett (1999) suggested, and as we will show below.

Most corporate universities have been 'closed', in the sense that they catered only for employees of the corporation, but now an increasing number are becoming more open – the Civil Service College in the UK now offers over 500 courses per annum to managers in other private and public organizations. Consequently, they are now both competitors and potential partners to those educational institutions that offer human resource-type programmes, and especially those that have geared a lot of their work towards industry and commerce. In the USA, Boston University, for instance, created Boston University Corporate Education Center (BUCEC) in 1988 to offer the types of training programmes that companies require and which the corporate universities now also offer. Many other universities have established similar centres. However, while corporate universities are obviously not competing with the arts and humanities programmes of normal universities, they are still exerting pressure on the curricula of the more traditional universities with which they are in partnership, and through the learning market on universities with which they have no partnership agreements, orientating them more directly to the interests of the corporate world.

In this chapter, we will examine the corporate universities, looking first at their history and expansion, then at their characteristics and programmes and, finally, we will seek to evaluate them as universities.

The history and expansion of the corporate university

It is difficult to trace a simple history of the corporate universities since many corporations started their own in-house education and training long before any of them thought of calling the establishments that they had created 'corporate universities'. In addition, some corporations, such as Arthur D Little, started their education and training to service the needs of their clients around the world rather than to train their own workforce.

A front-end model of training, rather like the front-end model of curriculum in education (Jarvis, 1995, p 26), was assumed by industry and commerce until about the 1960s. Thereafter, different curricular models emerged, as did different patterns of education and training. Corporations started their own in-house training schools while they were also sending their staff to more traditional education institutions. By the early 1960s the large corporations were seeing a need for their own training schools – but even here it is difficult to document their history. Meister (1998, p 210), for instance, suggests that McDonald's Hamburger University was formed in 1963, whereas Schugurensky (WWW) claims that it was 1961 (see McDonald's, WWW). Schugurensky goes on to state that Hamburger University is now a 130,000 square feet state-of-the-art facility and that it trained 65,000 managers during its first four decades of existence. There is a 22-language simultaneous translation facility at Hamburger University, which claims to be the largest training institution in the USA – even larger than the US army. It also has a further 10 international centres. Despite all of these facilities, Crainer (WWW) suggests rather sceptically that there are only 30 resident professors, but then we would expect it to employ more part-time teachers since this is a dominant employment pattern at the present time.

Gradually, during the years following the creation of Hamburger University, more corporations established their own education and training facilities, and some scholars were beginning to examine the process (Casner-Lotto and Associates, 1988; Eurich, 1985; Willis and Dubin, 1990, *inter alia*). These books tended to report case studies of different corporations and the way in which they were developing their own education and training facilities. Eurich (1985, p 48) also recorded the fact that by the time she was writing, there were approximately 400 companies in the USA that had their own learning centres, many of which were called universities. This figure has grown rapidly, and by 1995 there were over 1,000 corporate universities and corporate training budgets totalled $52 billion – and increase of 15 per cent since 1990 (Rowley, Lujan and Dolence 1998, p 34). (As mentioned in the previous chapter, the exact amount of money spent on training in the USA appears to be something of an estimate.) In the UK, there have been similar developments – such as the British Aerospace Virtual University, the University of Lloyds TSB, and other major companies having their own training centres, academies and so forth. By 1998, it was estimated by Corporate University Xchange Inc that there would be 2000 such institutions by the year 2000 with smaller companies taking the initiative.

Kenny-Wallace (2000, p 61) claims that:

> Traditional universities are no longer the dominant players in the creation and communication of knowledge, especially in cyberspace. Just-in-case education has moved to just-in-time and just-for-you, as self-managed computer-based learning plays an increasing and natural role for individuals and families. What to teach, how to learn and issues of quality are topical again. Plato.com has arrived.

Corporate universities have not just arrived in the USA and the UK; they are to be found in countries throughout Europe and Asia. In 1998, Daimler-Benz claimed to be the first company in Germany to establish a corporate university, but other companies rapidly followed suit. In France, France Telecom University uses an intranet to organize 160 training sessions a week for its 140,000 employees. In Canada, Sierra Systems launched its online university on 16 June 2000, designed to meet the career development of its own 900 staff. In Singapore in the summer of 2000, there was a conference for corporate universities in Asia, as there was in London in October of the same year for those in Europe. In addition, two different corporate universities were advertising for staff in Cape Town in the same week in October. Indeed, not only is it not difficult to find corporate universities at the turn of the century, it is not hard to examine their mission statements, since many advertise them on the Internet. In retrospect, in a knowledge society these developments should not be regarded as particularly surprising.

A number of corporate universities do not only offer training for their company's own employees. Motorola, among others, expects its supply and distribution chains to participate in its programmes, and its university is also involved in the hiring of employees and with working with those agencies likely to refer potential employees to the corporation. Motorola requires all of its associates (employees) to undertake 40 hours a year of job-relevant education in one of its seven learning centres around the world, through which it also offers a consulting and training service both internally and externally. It employs a workforce of 400 professionals and 700 writers, developers, translators and instructors. In addition, it is expected to be a money-earner rather than a cost on the company.

Meister (1994, p 22) suggested that:

> The goal has become to instill the entire chain with an understanding of the company's quality vision as well as a passion to continuously learn, so that learning happens as a part of an individual's job, either at a computer work station, working with a team of suppliers, in customer forums, or alone via a self-paced workbook or audio/videotape. The emphasis on promoting a spirit of continuous lifelong learning is what makes Corporate Quality Universities so different from the traditional corporate classrooms of the past decade.

Other corporates have targeted their clientele even more widely:

> The Iams Company, a $300 million privately held company serving the premium pet food market, has developed Iams University specifically to provide training to business channel members, including pet store owners, distributors, veterinarians and breeders. In fact Iams Company devotes 20 per cent of its training budget to train these independent distributors who supply Iams brands to pet speciality retailers worldwide. (Meiseter, 1998, p 45)

We can see that the education and training offered by these companies aims to ensure that the entire production and marketing of their products is undertaken by people they have trained.

As these corporate universities have come into existence, they have sought accreditation for their programmes. Eurich (1985, p 85) found:

> A new development on the scene of business and education is the growing number of corporate colleges, institutes, or universities that grant their own academic degrees. It is the Rand PhD, the Wang or Arthur D Little Master of Science degree. No longer the purview of established educational institutions alone, accredited academic degrees are being awarded increasingly by companies and industries

that have created their own separate institutions and successfully passed the same educational hurdles used to accredit traditional higher education.

By 1985, Eurich had discovered 18 institutions offering academic qualifications at associate, bachelors, Master's and doctoral level. The first academic award was offered as early as 1945. However, the concept of level requires considerable discussion. She went on to make the following significant point:

> All 18 corporate institutions operate what may be called an 'open admissions' policy. They are, quite literally, open to all qualified persons *outside* the sponsoring corporation. While this is literally true, one exception requires notice: McDonald's Hamburger University basically only serves its own employees, but it admits students from its supplier organizations and has perhaps eight or so a year.
>
> The important point is that these are not typically 'in-house' educational programs for employees. The Rand, Wang and Arthur D Little institutes do not serve employees of their parent organizations; each admits students who meet the admissions requirements from any college or university, any company, or from any country. Their graduates cannot expect employment by the sponsoring firm. (Eurich, 1985, p 97, emphasis in the original)

These are, then, universities approaching a more traditional mode but founded by the corporations. Now there are far more corporate universities accredited to offer academic qualifications. Indeed, by June 1999 the Jones International University, which calls itself the University of the Web, was advertising that it was the first fully online accredited university: accredited by the North Central Association of Colleges and Schools, which is responsible for the accreditation of all higher education institutions in its region.

Some of the programmes from the corporate quality universities are also getting college credit. Degree programmes are also beginning to emerge and a partnership between the American Express Quality University and Rio Salado Community College, for instance, has led to an associate degree in customer relations for American Express employees. The manager of the American Express Quality University said:

> We hope that if employees get college credit for training programs they complete, they will be more motivated to further their education and pursue two- or four-year degree programs as deemed appropriate for their jobs. (Cited by Meister, 1994, pp 162–63)

In the same way that American Express has linked itself to the Rio Salado Community College, other corporate universities are entering into partnerships and other associations with more traditional universities. Disney, for instance, links its name to Cornell University by pointing out that there are many alumni of the Disney College programme at Cornell and offering on the Internet intern opportunities for Cornell University students. Indeed, its alumni association is a registered student association of the University (www.rso.cornell.edu).

Despite the name 'university', which is not used by all corporate training institutions, not all of them are actually involved in highly sophisticated academic programmes. Many of the programmes appear to be at a further education or community college, rather than higher education, level. Indeed, the University of Lloyds TSB regards most of its work as being at this lower level (*THES,* 1999). But a clear distinction between these levels is now hard to maintain, so that in the UK they might well target foundation degree level work when that is fully established. The learning that occurs might be cognitive or practical or both; it might be personal or advantageous to the corporation as a whole; it might occur as a result of teaching or discovery. But it is not specifically restricted to any specific level of knowledge, and should be regarded as transferable. That corporate universities are seeking to offer academic-type qualifications indicates that they see themselves as being in the educational market (Baudrillard, 1988) and that they are seeking some form of academic respectability for what they do.

Characteristics and programmes of corporate universities

Corporate universities are many and various as they are being established to take their place in the learning market. Traditional universities should not be surprised at this growth, for it is yet another indicator of the success of the capitalist enterprise: wherever there is a gap in the market suppliers will seek to fill it. With the growth of the knowledge society, there were bound to be market-led organizations that would endeavour to take advantage of the lack of supply of easily accessible knowledge. Universities, with the notable exception of university extramural departments in the UK, and some colleges of further education, have not traditionally operated under these conditions and were in no shape to respond to the market – even if they should have done.

Consequently, it is hard to typify a corporate university since different ones have emerged to respond to different gaps in the market. We have such institutions as NoonTime University, Presenters University, Learn University and Coach U, to name but a few. These are private institutions claiming the corporate university title. NoonTime University is:

> for busy professionals who want training – but can't get away from work. Over 40 three-hour high-impact, interactive, tailored programs teach immediately applicable skills and are often wrapped around the lunch hour. (NoonTime University, WWW)

Presenters University and Coach U are just what they claim to be – offering courses in presentation style and coaching. Learn University 'creates customized Web-based training solutions for self-paced learning and live delivery over the Internet'. It claims that, 'Our professional instructors, designers, and technicians blend the science of learning, the art of design, and the latest in technology to create successful online instruction' (Learn University, WWW).

Almost without exception the corporate universities are using all forms of distance education as a means of marketing their programmes, from videotapes and study guides to Web-based courses and workstations. One of the driving forces of globalization is information technology and the corporates employ it all the time.

These four are small organizations that offer a single product, or a limited range of courses through convenient modes of delivery in a fast-growing market. They use the title 'university' because it is fashionable to do so and provides them with a good selling image. Additionally, we have to remember that words in American English and British English do not always have the same meaning, and the term 'university' has traditionally been less restrictive in the USA than in the UK. We will return to these institutions in the next chapter, but here we have to recognize that they are a completely different form of education and training organization to that offered by Motorola and McDonald's.

Castner-Lotto and Associates (1988, p 23) sought to isolate the essence of these latter universities, which she suggested was fourfold:

1. building a competency-based training curriculum for each job;
2. providing all employees with a common vision of the company;
3. extending training to the company's entire customer/supply chain;
4. serving as a learning laboratory for experimenting with new approaches and practices for the design and delivery of learning initiatives.

Chase (1998) suggested that corporate universities have seven functions. They:

1. teach corporate culture;
2. foster cross-functional skills;
3. utilize technology-based training;
4. cut cycle times;
5. operate training as a line of business;
6. educate outsiders;
7. develop partnerships with traditional universities.

Thus it can be seen that these institutions are designed to respond quickly to corporate needs and to make a financial return to the company by operating in a learning market. It should be noted that issues of quality and regulation do not feature among these functions, although some corporate universities claim to be extremely concerned about quality (Motorola.com, WWW), and Meister (1994) called them 'corporate quality universities' in the first edition of her book – although she dropped 'quality' from the title of the second (1998) edition.

Many of the corporate universities are now offering a consultancy service and assume two other roles: developing business plans and measuring whether the company achieves its goal. In a sense, this latter function might be considered to be an early stage in the development of research into corporate processes. However, Motorola University's mission statement certainly does not include research in quite such an explicit manner:

> The University's mission is to be a catalyst for change and continuous improvement in support of the corporation's business objectives. We will provide our clients in leading edge training and education solutions and systems to be their preferred partner in developing a Best Class workforce. (Motorola.com, WWW)

The workers being educated in the corporate universities need to be able to do and to know, so that teaching abstract theory has disappeared to a great extent and practical knowledge lies at the heart of the curricula. Programmes have been designed for their function within the company, concentrating on aspects of education and training that would have traditionally been the preserve of further education but also straddling the divide between it and higher education. Each module is specifically designed for a particular job or procedure, based in practice. It is summed up with the 'three Cs' of the core curriculum (Meister, 1998, pp 88–129):

- corporate citizenship – know how the company works, and its values and vision;
- contextual framework – know the company's customers, competitors and their best practices;
- competencies – know and practise both established and new job competencies.

Each of these three categories has a number of subdivisions that illustrate the extent to which the corporate universities offer a programme relevant to the corporations within which they function. Nearly all are practical and knowledge-based and at the heart of the competencies required are:

- learning to learn skills;
- communication skills;
- creative thinking and problem solving;
- technological literacy;
- global business literacy;
- leadership skills.

Each of these is a core skill for the business world. All workers should be learners all the time and this underlies the idea that the corporate quality university should be a learning laboratory. One of the faculties in the British Aerospace Virtual University is the Faculty of Learning. Learning rather than teaching lies at the heart of these new universities.

The fact that corporations are now using the language of civil democracy and talking about corporate citizenship is itself a significant feature, indicating that global capitalism is now assuming a new discourse – one that is foreign to its nature. Meister (1998, pp 95–98) describes how the transnational companies not only utilize the language of citizenship but train new employees in corporate citizenship, rather like the Americanization and Canadianization programmes in the education of immigrants in the early 20th century (see Carlson, 1987). However, these latter programmes were training into a national culture whereas the corporate ones are training into the corporate culture, and through a hidden curriculum into a global capitalist culture. Meister (1998, p 97) writes:

> The companies with corporate universities make a deliberate attempt, through formal course offerings in the company's values, culture and history, as well as technology-based tools, to develop a strong sense of corporate citizenship among all members of the workforce.

She quotes (1998, p 95) the director of the University of Chicago Hospital:

> Our vision in creating the orientation program for UCH was to develop a program where our employees could learn to be good citizens. To us, a good citizen moves beyond performing just the job tasks. Rather a good citizen acts like he/she is the owner of the business, desires to satisfy customers, understands that customer satisfaction comes from how the job is done, and takes responsibility for continually striving to do a better job.

Employable individuals can become corporate citizens; even though they do not own the business they can act in its interests, as if they do. They are educated to be active and corporate citizens in furthering the corporate mission, while they may well remain passive and private citizens in the sphere of the activities of the state itself, although there are some instances where corporate training has resulted in more active citizenship at state level. Active and 'public' citizenship within the corporation means that the citizens are actually no more than human resources who can further the aims (mission) of the company. Their 'ownership' of the job is but a temporary expediency by the corporation and they can lose their citizenship as soon as they are redundant to the company's requirements within the global or local markets. Globalization is, consequently, beginning to redefine citizenship and restrict it in line with the reduction of welfare services in weak states.

To illustrate the types of course offered by the corporate universities, the following two lists are taken from Motorola University's Web site. Its course catalogue consists of the following two sections – topics and personnel who might be interested. The courses are offered to Motorola employees, their chains of supply and distribution and to a wider clientele.

Interest categories:

- corporate university/training;
- cycle time reduction/cross-functional process mapping;
- empowerment/team building;
- finance;
- history;
- management/leadership development;
- personnel development;
- quality/six sigma;
- strategic planning/business needs analysis.

Functional categories:

- customer services;
- engineering support;
- management;
- manufacturing management and supervision;
- manufacturing technicians;
- quality;
- sales, marketing and distribution;
- software engineering;
- technical sales.

Perhaps the only term that needs clarification in this list is 'six sigma', which refers to the signs of success of the company: increased productivity; higher quality product; elimination of product defects during production; lowering manufacturing costs; growth in revenues and stock prices. The University refers to this high level of functioning as having achieved a 'Black Belt' level of expertise, which is more indicative of skills training than of academic development.

It should be pointed out that in traditional universities, modularization is a process of breaking down a topic into a number of discrete entities with a study time lasting from about 25 hours to 300–400 hours. By contrast, the corporate universities break down the job for which they offer training into discrete entities and offer training, only now the time spent learning that aspect of the job might take minutes and not hours.

Motorola also offers full-day training seminars for executives, starting with a 7.30 am breakfast and finishing at 5 pm, and among the topics offered in 1998 were:

- Globalization.
- Leadership.
- Motorola Quality & Time Cycle Reduction Stories.
- Customer Focused Quality.
- Education & Development for Leaders.
- Teaming.
- Reward & Recognition.
- How a Global Company Communicates with its Employees.
- Quality and the Bottom Line.
- Leading Continuous Improvement.
- How to Lead an Organization During Rapid Change.

Most of the areas in the above curricula are also ones in which Motorola University offers consultancy services. Consultancy itself should be regarded by the traditional universities as an educative function, as these corporate universities do. It is clearly another way of capitalizing on the residual expertise in the corporate university.

Despite the use of electronic means of communication for most of its courses, it is also significant that Motorola University now has its own publishing press – Motorola University Press. Of all the corporate universities, Motorola has moved a considerable way down the pathway to producing a new model of the university on an international scale.

In a rapidly changing global market the corporate universities have found a place where the traditional universities find it difficult to gain a foothold. As Eurich (1985) showed, the traditional universities move at a too leisurely pace for the corporates. Ahrens University in Sweden provides an example of the way that corporate universities respond to the global market. Founded in 1997 as the University of Rapid Growth (UniRap) with the aim of doubling the number of 'Swedish hyper-growing companies', it ran its first management course in March 1997. It ran a number of management programmes and as a result of the third one, it joined forces with Ericsson and Telia to create Business Creators in 1999. The following year it was not only running management and business creators programmes, but it also started e-Market Creators and changed its name to Ahrens University. By 2000, it was claiming on its Web site (ahrensuniversity.com):

> We are constantly trying to locate and evaluate new and rapidly growing fields of business, in order to package this knowledge in faculties and programmes. You can be certain that you will soon hear of further hyper-growth-focused training facilities, labelled with the name 'Ahrens University'.

Corporate universities are a response to the market of the learning society – they have become essential elements of companies that seek to compete in the global market. Clearly they are very different from traditional universities, and so it is now necessary to look critically at their claim to be universities.

Corporate universities as universities

In order to begin to understand the place of corporate universities within education it is necessary to understand both the concepts of university and higher education, neither of which is easy to define in the contemporary world. Barnett (1990, 1994, 1997, 2000) has arguably devoted more time than others to explore these problems and naturally over the decade he has changed and modified his work in the light of changes in society. His formulation might also help to evaluate the corporate universities as universities, or at least, as institutions of higher education.

Barnett has suggested a two-fold formulation of competence: operational and academic. He viewed operational competence as *knowledge how:* pragmatic, outcomes-orientated, concerned with transferability of procedures, experiential, strategic, economic, organizational and aimed at better practical effectiveness (1994, p 160). When we look at the claims of the corporate universities, we see that these are precisely the bases on which they make their claims.

The corporate universities are concerned with operational competence, so that they are able to perform their role, at whatever level they work. It will be recalled that Motorola University offered a whole list of functional categories. Indeed, one list of benefits claimed by the corporate university of DeSai Systems (1999, p 1) is:

- Enhancement of productivity and organizational impact.
- Learning solutions.
- Elimination of duplicate efforts and wasted resources.
- Training measured against business objectives.
- Reduced administrative costs.
- Long-life learning environment.
- Improved employee satisfaction.
- Linking training to job performance.
- Employee recognition of the relationship between technology training and career advancement.

In examining the claims made by and about many corporate universities it is clear that their main concern is with operational competence, although they are keen to show that they are linked to academic organizations that profess their own form of academic competence. Barnett (1994, p 160) suggested that these include *knowledge that:* disciplinary, prepositional, seeking truthfulness and cognitive. Overall, these characteristics are not to be found among the claims of the corporate universities, with the possible exceptions of such skills as self-directed learning and strategic planning.

In a more recent book, Barnett (2000, pp 104–09) refines his (1994, p 179) categorization 'life world becoming', which for him was the essence of 'beyond competence'. Now, in an age of super-complexity, he suggests six conditions of 'realizing the university':

1. critical interdisciplinarity;
2. collective self-scrutiny;
3. purposive renewal;
4. moving borders;
5. engagement;
6. communicative tolerance.

He rightly recognizes these as features of an ideal type that will never actually be realized, but one of the functions of utopianism is always to register that what has been achieved is only a stage in the process to something better. In the final section of this last book, he returns to the three fundamental functions of the university – administration, research and teaching, and it remains significant that service does not appear crucial to his thinking about the nature of the university. Even so, we feel that universities in the UK have traditionally performed a service function to their local community, although they have never publicized it in quite the same way as have the US universities. Consequently, we feel that it is not beyond reason to suggest four basic functions of the university: administration, research, teaching and service.

Taking these last four elements first, we can see immediately that corporate universities only provide a teaching function, although they may be beginning to undertake certain forms of research into process knowledge and they see themselves as providing a service to their relevant corporate interests. The corporate universities are usually managed by the corporation, the company undertakes most of the research into content knowledge and if it provides service to the local community it is often in the form of well-publicized sponsorships. In fact the whole of the knowledge-intensive corporation is more likely to fulfil the functions of the university than does the corporate university, although even here its areas of concern are much more restricted and its borders are more closed than those of the traditional university.

This brings us to Barnett's six conditions of the university and we shall examine each in turn:

1. *Critical interdisciplinarity* means that all forms of disciplinary inquiry need to give account of themselves, be reflexive and seek to understand and appreciate the contribution that they all make to the collective good. This will result in debate and dialogue between the disciplines so that the university can be seen to be holding together the total universe of knowledge. Perhaps Barnett's claim is a little too sweeping since universities are no longer the sole producers of knowledge. Even so, corporate universities could not currently see themselves as contributing a great deal to this debate.

2. *Collective self-scrutiny* means that universities have the responsibility to engage in open debate about the nature and purpose of the university. Barnett recognizes that this is something that universities have not done, whereas corporate universities know precisely why they exist. The reasons for their existence may be limited and uncritical; nevertheless, they exist but they are not really collective enterprises and they are certainly not critical.

3. *Purposive renewal* means that universities need to know not only why they exist but also how they can continue to renew and reform themselves in the light of the social pressures that they experience. Barnett (2000, p 106) makes the point that unless they do they will 'become a shuttlecock buffeted by global capitalism'. A major part of the argument of this book is that the universities have already become buffeted by global capitalism and are becoming more like the corporates that control the corporate universities, since they are no longer certain about what they actually are.

4. *Moving borders* means that both the epistemological and the structural borders need to be more flexible. Whether the ways that universities are restructuring themselves are the most beneficial to the future of the university is certainly a debateable question as Aronovitz (2000) argues, although it appears to be a muted debate at present, while the epistemological restructuring is harder to achieve since academics are wedded to the traditional disciplines. Corporate universities have never had to face epistemological restructuring since they are contemporary institutions dealing with the forms of knowledge that the corporates need and their management structures are contained by the nature of corporate capitalism.

5. *Engagement* means that the universities have to engage with a variety of different communities. No longer can it be seen to be an ivory tower, although Barnett (2000, p 109) cites the Dearing Report in the UK, which reaffirms that universities should be 'the conscience of society'. Barnett suggests that this ideal is not possible but that universities should become 'sites of the production of multiple and *contending* perspectives'. We have seen, however, that because universities are not ivory towers, they are exposed to the economic power structures of capitalist society and have had large sponsorships withdrawn because they have entertained perspectives other than those of the corporations concerned. If universities are to engage with the wider society, they do need either a degree of freedom or to recognize that they are liable to face considerable economic pressure from the corporate world. This is a debate in which the universities need to engage but one which the corporate universities cannot even envisage.

6. *Communicative tolerance* means that universities need to maximize the opportunities for different voices to be heard and in this sense should become a forum for democratic society. Once again this is not the type of forum that corporate universities have been established to provide.

Overall, it can be seen that using Barnett's analyses of the concept of the university, the corporate universities do not appear to measure up. This means that Barnett is completely wrong, or the corporate universities are completely wrong to claim to be universities, or the term 'university' is being used in a different manner. Since nobody would now claim that there is actually an agreed meaning to the concept university, we can rule out the first two of these suggestions, although we appreciate that Barnett's analyses come closer to what is generally perceived to be the university. Therefore, we need to ask ourselves why the corporations did not continue to regard their centres of education and training as just centres of excellence in education and training for a knowledge society.

In the first instance, we have to appreciate that the idea of the corporate university emanated from the USA, where universities have had a tradition both of service to the local community, and especially through the Land Grant colleges, of service to local community agriculture and industry. This makes them markedly different in their orientations than certain British universities. Secondly, pragmatism is more fundamental to the US university system than it is to the European universities, so that there has always been a slightly different emphasis on the types of knowledge valued. Thirdly, American English does not carry the same connotations as does British English about the concept of the 'university', since it has functioned within a mass higher education system for a much longer period than the UK. The term 'university' consequently carries the connotation of forms of education that are not school education.

In addition, corporations were emphasizing the need for learning and communication skills, things that young people were not taught sufficiently during their schooling. These were skills that they could obtain in community colleges in the USA, which often offered two-year degree programmes. Community colleges offer practical skills courses and beginning higher education, and they are sometimes referred to as universities. At the same time, the term 'university' still carries a perception of something good and to be desired, a form of post-school education, which corporations in the contemporary world could latch on to, and so the term seemed less strange there when they called their centres of excellence 'universities'. Meister (1998, pp 34–35) claims that:

The companies that have packaged their learning and development programs under the corporate university model have decided the university approach conjured up the sort of expectations that matched their objectives. They wanted a strategic umbrella to systematize the training effort, centralize its design, development and administration, apply consistent measures, become a 'new product laboratory' for experimenting with new ways for employees to learn, and reap the cost efficiencies of a shared service model of delivering education. More importantly, they wanted the university metaphor to provide the image for the grand intent of the initiative: promising participants and their sponsors that the corporate university will prepare them for success in the current and future career.

They actually compete with community colleges in the United States. Rowley et al 1998, pp 158–59) write about the growth of corporate universities:

> This growth has not only broadened the scope of corporate educa-tion, but it has also helped to shape it. As more and more of these companies have expressed concerns about the quality of the educa-tion their new employees bring with them from colleges and universities... several of these companies have begun to structure their own educational programs to rival those acquired on college and university campuses. Several are saying that they would prefer to educate their employees from the beginning of a college career themselves rather than have to re-educate employees who do not come to them with language, mathematical, social, managerial, or computer preparation the companies believe they should have received in their college preparation.

Consequently, we can see that corporate universities locate themselves within the framework of community colleges and two-year degree programmes, rather like the proposed foundation degree in British higher education. They see themselves as supplementing school education and training and providing continuing education for employees. Indeed, when Lloyds TSB established its own corporate university in the UK (*THES,* 1999), it claimed that most of its work would be in further education, although it is difficult to demarcate them now. Corporate universities are perhaps closer rivals to colleges of further and higher education than they are to the British universities, although they will compete with them at the points where the programmes overlap and duplicate each other. At the same time, we might expect that they will seek academic accreditation, so that they will become greater rivals in the learning market in the not too distant future.

They are, however, essentially education and training establishments that will lead to a form of capitalist cultural reproduction rather than centres of democratic criticality, that we might expect from the more traditional university. They perhaps run the risk, by using the term university, of confusing further with higher education – but then there are now no more borders, as the title 'colleges of further and higher education' implies.

It can be seen from this discussion that corporate education might entail both content and process knowledge, but the extent to which it actually offers an all-round education is another question. Additionally, traditional universities do well to examine the corporate universities with a great deal of critical awareness before they recognize them as offering the same educational service as they do. This is not to say, however, that corporate universities might not grow and develop in precisely the same way as other private universities and extend their curricula in the future if they find that they are engaged in a profitable enterprise.

Conclusion

In this chapter we have discussed four totally different types of institution that might be called a corporate university:

1. University business schools and centres orientated to corporate needs.
2. University–business partnerships.
3. Universities established by corporations.
4. Private universities and business schools orientated to corporate needs.

Within each of these types there are a number of sub-types. They can all be classified under this umbrella term, which reflects the dominance of global capitalism, and they all constitute part of the learning market that we shall discuss in the next chapter. At the same time, we have raised some doubts about corporate universities as actually being universities in the sense that this is traditionally assumed, even though we recognize that they benefit from the title. Indeed, they might be new types of university, since the term itself is assuming a different meaning, and the universities founded by the corporations might be new types of university, in the same way as civic universities were when they were founded by the state and local governments in previous centuries.

8

The lifelong learning industry

The thesis of this book has been that education, especially university education, has been forced to respond to the pressures of globalization and where it has failed to do so adequately, corporations have started their own education and training centres, some of which are now known as corporate universities. As part of this thesis it has also been argued that the learning society is a learning market in which the established educational institutions no longer enjoy anything like a monopoly; it was suggested that distance education provided one of the easiest ways of marketing education and that the British Open University had been a major catalyst in the development of this process. Indeed, to continue to use the market metaphor, educational institutions are both manufacturers and providers (on the supply side of the market) of knowledge.

Learning materials, learning packages, study guides and so on, have become commodities that have to be sold and learners are the purchasers, or even the consumers of the product. The award is the symbol by which they were offered on the market – the MBA, BSc and the UK's NVQ – all appear in advertisements trying to persuade people that they need to purchase the learning materials, and the slogan 'Learning is Fun' has appeared all over the place. Of course it is – sometimes – but it is also hard work and stress inducing, phenomena not mentioned anywhere in the advertising. Learning is also the motor of human growth and development and, not surprisingly, this is not mentioned in these terms although there are many places where the idea of human growth and development are implied. The certificate of successful completion becomes the receipt of purchase. Learning then becomes a form of consumption in the consumer society, as Featherstone (1991, p 19), cited in Chapter 5 on page 87, outlines.

Educational institutions are gradually adjusting to the idea that they are suppliers of learning materials ('providers' is a term that has been in frequent use in the education of adults for many decades), and that the learning material is the commodity that contains the information that can become knowledge, which might also become intellectual capital, or even social capital, for the purchaser. Knowledge production is now part of a manufacturing industry; an industry is a commercial enterprise concerned with the output of a specified commodity or service. But for most producers, there is a competitive market in which to sell those products, and few universities have been exposed to such a competitive market before in their history.

Indeed, the only branch of education that has been established on anything like market principles has been the education of adults. In the 1980s, for instance, there was a debate in the US adult education literature as to whether adult education would be better centralized and controlled or left to the free market (Peters and Associates, 1980). Griffith (1980, pp 78–114) suggested that the programmes should be coordinated, whereas Knowles (1980, pp 12–40) considered that it was best left to the market to respond to whatever demands there were for education. Knowles (1980, p 39) wrote:

> Clearly the adult education function of most institutions is moving from the peripheral status it occupied for so long toward a more central status. Indeed, institutions of higher education are moving away from being almost exclusively youth-serving organizations to becoming almost predominantly adult-serving organizations. Meanwhile, the system is demonstrating a high degree of creativity in its ability to invent new institutional forms – residential centers, external degree programs, clearinghouses, brokering agencies, and the like – to meet new needs.

Knowles was clearly right – adult education enterprises have responded to the demands of the market in a multitude of different ways, with a wide variety of new approaches appearing since he wrote these words. Universities, however, have struggled with the changes that have been forced upon them. Perhaps then it is necessary to turn briefly to the education of adults to try to map the field in which universities are struggling to find their place.

Apps (1989, pp 275–86), in seeking to map the field of providers of education for adults in the USA, suggested four separate categories:

1. Agencies that are fully or partially tax-supported – eight types specified.
2. Non-profit agencies that are self-supporting – eight types specified.
3. For-profit providers – 11 types specified.
4. Non-organized learning opportunities – five types specified.

As a result of his survey, Apps concluded that there was a blurring between adult and higher education and he showed how higher educational institutions were offering an increasing number of degree programmes in evenings and weekends and through electronic means of delivery. He also included some of the corporate training centres in his analysis of for-profit providers, although he clearly did not see them as tremendously significant to adult education. In adult education in the USA, generally, at that time, there was less concern with what was going on in industry and commerce, with the notable exception of Houle (1980), and so the idea of a learning market does not feature strongly in the literature. However, the Carnegie Foundation for the Advancement of Teaching was more aware of the situation, and in 1990 Eurich published *The Learning Industry* in which she examined the continuing professional education provision of many different corporations.

Obviously the concern of educators in the past has been the nature of learners, eg gender, age, socio-economic class, since it has been assumed that individuals would be the students, although it was beginning to be recognized that a number of the students would be sponsored by their employers. Once sponsorship begins to occur, however, the students cease to be the clients of the educational provider – the sponsoring agency becomes the client. It would have been instructive, in retrospect, for any educational institution that supplied these educational programmes to have analysed who the sponsoring employers were and what types of programmes they were sponsoring their employees to follow. But already there were indications that the traditional educational institutions could not change sufficiently rapidly to respond to the demands that those sponsors were making and so we have witnessed the rapid development of the corporate universities.

The world of business and industry had been changed by the forces of globalization, and the knowledge society had been born. Now the global substructure needed both to research and to disseminate knowledge. It was concerned with both content and process knowledge, since it needed to produce commodities efficiently at competitive market rates in order to survive. Now the boundaries have been destroyed, the sponsors and consumers of knowledge have become the producers and manufacturers of knowledge and, at the other end of the spectrum, the providers of knowledge are trying to market the commodities that can be created from the knowledge that they have produced. There is now no clear demarcation of providers and consumers: in different situations each performs different functions. But there is an adult learning industry.

It would, consequently, be impossible to produce a similar map of the market to that which Apps produced at the end of the 1980s, and no attempt to do so will be undertaken here. However, we will look briefly at the place of the universities and the corporate universities in the learning industry at the present time.

The corporate universities

We have seen that the corporate universities have been established to provide knowledge for their own companies and the corporation's supply and distribution chains. Once they have extended their markets in this way, it is a small step for them to offer education and training opportunities for a wider clientele. Indeed, some corporations prefer to train their own employees in any case, so that this step has already been encouraged by some companies. This becomes even more compelling once the corporate universities are expected to become financially self-sufficient. Meister (1998, p 53) writes:

> First, Moore (Director of SunU of Sun Microsystems) believes adopting a totally self-funded model requires that a corporate university's customers drive the training agenda and vote with their dollars. A 100 per cent self-funded model means the corporate university implements and sustains only those programs and courses that solve real business problems. Second, the corporate university reduces its course offerings because it eliminates courses that are nice but not central to business unit needs. SunU eliminated about 40 per cent of the courses it offered in 1995 because they were not addressing the strategic needs of Sun employers. Finally, the implementation of a self-funded business model avoids the danger of becoming isolated from customers and reduces the need to construct elaborate return on investment models to justify one's existence within the corporation.

SunU is by no means the only corporate university that is expected to be self-funded but once this occurs, we can see that the corporate universities are not only going to be partners of the traditional universities and colleges of further and higher education, they are also going to be competitors in the business of producing programmes that will sell in the learning marketplace. However, this does not restrict the corporate universities just to their corporations' main area of business – once they have become business organizations in their own right, there is not reason why they should not supply a wider range of courses, if they are profitable, especially to the young adults who have completed their initial education and are seeking a way into employment. Some corporations, critical of the mainstream education system,

The Lifelong Learning Industry 133

might well find it profitable to have their own corporate universities prepare the next generation of employees for them – and then for other corporations as well. Hence a number of corporate universities are seeking academic accreditation for their courses. In the future it may be only in those less profitable areas that the corporations might seek to sponsor employees on courses offered by the more traditional providers of education, or on those highly specialized ones – such as postgraduate programmes – that few of the corporate universities will be able to provide in the first instance.

Significantly, we have seen that many of the corporate universities offer a consultancy service. In a sense, consultancy is an educative function that is part of the learning industry. Consultancy is not just management consultancy: it is all forms of consultancy, including human resource development, marketing and production and so on. In providing a consultancy service, the corporate universities are also undertaking practical research and, it should be recalled, it is these large companies that have stored and manage vast amounts of practical knowledge about their operations worldwide. As they have this knowledge, so they are able to offer advice to governments and transnational corporations on very many aspects of economic life, and governments are utilizing and paying for their expertise – however well researched their consultancy knowledge might, or might not, actually be.

Another aspect of the corporate university side of this industry has emerged in recent years. As corporate universities have become more fashionable, so a number of private companies have been established that offer to create a corporate university for the corporation. One such company is SRI International, which claims that in establishing a corporate university, it includes the following issues in its considerations:

- development of a 'brand' or identity for the university, to secure stakeholder buy-in and utilization;
- selection of a strategy governing the mix of traditional versus Web-based delivery;
- analysis of financing options, including commercialization of content and delivery approaches to generate revenue;
- resolution of oversight, maintenance, and organizational 'ownership' responsibilities including the degree of centralization/decentralization;
- consideration of alliances, particularly with degree-granting academic institutions (a growing trend);
- use of the corporate university to achieve non-training objectives, such as the promotion of corporate culture and mission (a need spurred by the increase of acquisitions and mergers). (sri.com, WWW)

In precisely the same way, ePath Learning offers six easy steps to creating a corporate university and this is to be found within the frameworks of the organization's own Buildkit and ManageKit (epathlearning, WWW) programmes. Indeed, ePath Learning claims that if the corporation has the training content, it has the tools to develop, deliver and manage that content over the Web, that is the process knowledge. Other organizations, such as Corporate Systems Incorporated, Corporate University Emplacement Program, Executive Knowledge Works and Mentergy are all involved in helping corporations establish their own corporate universities. These are new forms of educational consultancies, dealing both with the corporations' own education and training needs and also with the delivery systems for these programmes, usually through the Internet.

It was the importance of the Internet that caused Duderstadt (1999) to ask: can the colleges and universities survive in an information age? One of the estimates made was that by the late 1990s, the converged forces supporting the delivery of interactive media to the home would be \$1 trillion (1993 dollar rate) (Katz, 1999, p 34) and Duderstadt was doubtful whether the traditional universities could respond to this huge market effectively. Katz, (1999, p 28) also observed that:

> Most colleges and universities will deliver some portion of their instructional offerings via communication networks. As these networks create the potential for global university outreach across significant elements of higher education's mission, course content and intellectual property holdings will become scarce economic goods and will command an economic premium.

While this is a positive answer to the question raised by Duderstadt, it does point to the fact that the traditional universities have got to consider carefully their strategies about the mode of delivery for their programmes, but it also underlines the value of knowledge in contemporary society.

One other point needs to be borne in mind when we consider the way in which education and training appear to be taking off through the Internet – many Internet companies failed in 2000, and since we are looking at education and training as an industry in a competitive market, there is no reason why many of the weaker dot.com companies offering education and training solutions should be any different from any of the other weaker electronic companies since they are exposed to the same market forces. Naturally, the stronger ones will survive, but that is the law of the market – although the stronger ones are not always the best!

The universities

The universities have struggled in the face of all these changes, which has caused all the discontent mentioned in the first chapter and resulted in a voluminous literature on the universities in crisis. Change nearly always does cause stress to the employees of the organization, especially when it is clear that the leaders of the sector have no better idea of the way forward than do most of the employees within it. But then we do live in a risk society, in which Beck (1992) makes the point that solutions are implemented to problems before we can know if they are the correct ones, continually causing the actors to reconsider the original 'solutions' to the problems. Universities are forced to be reflexive organizations, if they are to embrace change, so that it often appears that cautiousness is safe and that when mistakes are apparently made, blame can be attributed to one or more individuals. But mistakes might merely be innovations that did not work at the time and the reason might not be the innovation but the system's failure to adapt to it sufficiently comprehensively. Safety may not be the way forward for the learning organization, as Senge (1990) suggested. Safety might actually be the long-term mistake and those who control the system might be as much to blame as the innovator, if blame is to be cast, but that may also be a mistake! It may be that the system needs to change a part, or all of the way in which it functions. However, there are many things that universities do well – even under stress conditions – and so this comment is not to suggest that the whole system is wrong. Even so, we are living in a world in which universities are exposed to the forces of globalization, in precisely the same manner as are the corporations and their universities, and in this world change is endemic.

What then is the universities' market? Traditionally, it has been young adults, school leavers, destined for the professions and elite of society. But with the advent of the knowledge society, a first degree may now be the entry qualification into many knowledge-based forms of employment; in the past, it was school-leaving qualifications that would guarantee reasonable employment. Undergraduate education is now the end of initial education for many young adults, and this is being underlined in the UK with the introduction of the two-year foundation degree. Universities have to decide whether this is going to be a major area of their work in the future. Many universities might consciously make the decision to continue to take this route, especially where the foundation and first degrees lead to a professional qualification and almost automatic entry into employment. This is a strong market, despite the demographic structure of the country, especially as these universities can offer their programmes on a worldwide basis.

Focusing on undergraduate education does not rule out the idea that such universities should not be institutions of lifelong learning, since many employees who did not get an undergraduate degree through the traditional route might want to get one later in life, maybe as part of their employment – like the American Express agreement with the Rio Salado Community College which has led to an associate degree in customer relations.

Neither should such an emphasis on undergraduate education rule out these universities from being involved in postgraduate education, although it might not be regarded as the main focus of their work. Naturally, they will have other competitors, possibly including the corporate universities, but these latter universities would probably offer narrower and more specialized programmes.

In a sense, the status of the undergraduate degree has changed. In the past, graduation signified the end of education, but now it only signifies the end of initial education, and so many universities are offering only an extended form of initial education. At present most universities are involved in this area of work but while they are doing so they are also being forced to respond to the demands that the knowledge society is making upon them, which is the growing market for postgraduate education. Part of the stress and the crises described in the first chapter is due to universities trying to expand their market in all directions without expanding the numbers of academic staff sufficiently. Some universities might actually do well to focus on this sector of the market for which they are better equipped to offer education and training in a flexible manner.

Perhaps some universities will have to recognize that in the future higher education will begin after the first degree and that their place is to offer more of their programmes at postgraduate level, where they will continue to have a greater share of the market and where they certainly have more expertise. They may create more postgraduate schools and focus their teaching at the level of taught Master's and doctoral programmes.

While most of the demands for postgraduate taught courses and practitioner doctorates are, at present, coming from the world of work, universities would be unwise to forget that people used to working with knowledge every day might also wish to pursue high levels of academic work in their leisure time, especially after they retire. Extramural courses, which currently tend to be at undergraduate level or below, can be expected to expand at postgraduate level. Already we are seeing a few people undertaking PhD research as a leisure-time pursuit, and this trend can be expected to continue.

Not all educational institutions that are regarded as universities can concentrate on postgraduate work for a number of reasons, including the fact that they do not all have a large enough proportion of sufficient highly trained academic staff. But on a more practical level, if universities all concentrated on postgraduate work, it would lead to a decline in the amount of undergraduate courses being offered at a time when mass higher education is what the knowledge society demands. In addition, there might not be a sufficiently large market for them all to concentrate on the postgraduate level.

If the type of division posed here is followed, then universities will be substantially different from each other and have different educational products to market, but this would not necessarily be a bad thing. It has to be conceded, however, that fewer of the corporate universities are working at postgraduate level at the moment, although there are already some that do so (Eurich, 1985) and if gaps appear in this market, more corporate and other private universities might begin to introduce new programmes at higher levels to fill them.

It should be noted that the division suggested here is not one of teaching versus research universities, since this contains a restricted understanding of research. In contemporary society, as we pointed out in earlier chapters, research is broader than the traditional understanding of it. It can involve research into content knowledge, process knowledge, into practitioner understanding and action and so on – as well as 'blue skies' research. Consequently, both universities that concentrate on first degree teaching and those that emphasize postgraduate teaching should be involved in research in their own specialist areas. In addition, some forms of research might also be undertaken as part of all universities' service to the community.

Naturally, some universities might wish to spread their provision more equally over both undergraduate and postgraduate work, but this does call for very careful organizational programming and very sophisticated marketing techniques. Clearly, universities have to decide on the educational programme they are going to market and then produce it efficiently.

Universities remain the only knowledge-intensive organizations that seek to incorporate all branches of knowledge within their sphere of activities. This breadth is both an advantage and a disadvantage: an advantage because it enables the universities to operate in a larger market, but a disadvantage because they need more specialists in marketing in the various sectors in which they work. There is another danger and that is that they are slower to accredit their own courses because of their size and peer-reviewing procedures. Since universities are functioning in a very competitive market environment, their procedures need to be much more streamlined so that departments offering courses can move from the generation of the idea to the marketing of the programme in a matter of months rather than years. As Duderstadt (1999) signified, universities are not only competing in terms of content but in terms of process. Paradoxically, the content may be less problematic than the process and in a competitive market there needs to be investment in the process so that the production and marketing of the programmes are just-in-time and learner/client-specific.

An area of the learning industry that universities might expand is their own consultancy services. Universities have stored a great deal of knowledge and the intellectual capital of their staff is as great as any other knowledge-intensive organization in the majority of fields in which they operate. Consultancy is not just offering an educational advice service, it is a form of practical knowledge research and should be regarded in this light. Undertaking it enables universities to gather and store practical knowledge that will be useful in future activities.

Consequently, universities do need to know their markets in the different work/subject areas throughout the world in whatever areas they function, and then they should market their products efficiently. After all, they are part of a very rapidly expanding and diverse learning industry – but they remain more than an industrial enterprise; we will return to this in the final chapter.

At the same time, universities are functioning much more independently of government and so we can expect them to act in the same way as other corporations – there will be mergers, takeovers and so on. We can expect to see multinational (multi-campus) universities appearing with greater frequency and, thereafter, we will see the growth of transnational universities. But since most universities are public institutions partly funded by government, unlike the corporate universities, it is necessary for government to be fully aware of the processes that are occurring and, in partnership with the universities, to introduce funding strategies that both enable them to respond quickly to the demands of the market, and also to play different roles in the adult learning industry as appropriate. This calls for continued constructive dialogue and an informed understanding, but the issues of privatizing the universities to act freely in the market is a debate that needs a great deal more consideration. There is a very strong case indeed, as this book has shown, for universities remaining public institutions and continuing to perform service to the community – whether it is local, regional or national. It could also be argued that there is a place for both approaches.

Conclusion

It will be recalled that Apps (1989) identified another form of adult learning – non-organized learning; he mentions television and so on. Now the Internet offers a vast spread of non-organized learning opportunities. Hundreds and thousands of pages of material are freely available to anybody who has access to the Web. Once again, adult educators have led the way in seeking to understand and research those learners who have been self-directed. As early as 1961, Houle wrote *The Enquiring Mind;* thereafter some of his students were engaged in researching this area of learning, notably Tough (1972). For over a decade Long has organized a North American, and then International, Conference on Self-Directed Learning (see Long and Associates, 1998, for papers from this annual conference). Many are engaged in self-directed learning throughout their lives and this has led to universities accrediting prior experiential learning, even though they have not been the providers of the knowledge learnt. However, universities might have to recognize and respond to self-directed learning in many more innovative ways than merely accrediting it on completion.

Universities might have lost their monopoly of knowledge, but in the end the purpose of the university still remains knowledge. Our understanding of knowledge and its uses has changed, mainly as a result of globalization, and universities have to change their functions in order to respond to those social pressures that have been created. They have a greater coverage of knowledge than any of the corporate universities and a potentially greater spread of students. They retain a major role in the adult learning industry. They can, and should, be institutions of lifelong learning and lifelong education, but they do need to confront the changes that are occurring head-on and decide on precisely how they are going to respond to all the pressures that the global market is putting on them. It will remain a time of stress, as it is in many occupations currently, but if universities want to reverse the trend of being sidelined as Bauman (1992) has suggested, they have to embrace this new knowledge society and play their role within it – but how they do this is another matter. Perhaps this is the question that Barnett (2000, p 99) implies when he states that universities simply do not know 'what it is to *be* a university' (emphasis in the original). Indeed, it has been suggested here that there are many different forms of university and that more may be emerging, and so the supplementary question is – can we actually speak meaningfully about *the* university any longer?

9

What is the university?

In the previous chapters we have seen how globalization has generated a knowledge industry, of which the universities are but one part. We have also noted how they, like other educational institutions, have been slow to respond to external pressures and that this has enabled other providers to find their own niches in the learning market; such providers also seek to produce and sell learning materials to an increasingly educated public. The distinctive mission of the university seems to be disappearing among a multitude of other providers who would also see their end being knowledge provision. So, is the university any different from all of these other organizations? What makes it distinctive? What, then, is the university? These are questions that may have no answer in absolute terms.

For Newman, the end of the university was knowledge. There have been many formulations about the university since Newman wrote his famous treatise, most recently Barnett's (2000) studies of the university and higher education, but even he acknowledges that defining the university in this age of supercomplexity is not possible. Most of the statements made about the nature of the university are either ideal types, or ideological visions of what the university ought to be according to the authors who propose them. Barnett recognizes that sociological analyses of the university are necessary and he makes the point (2000, p 61) that all the stories about the university are suspect, while he is quite sure that the 'university no longer knows what it is to *be* a university' (p 99). But he also makes the point that in this super-complex world, the challenges are not ones of knowing but ones of being (p 164). But perhaps 'being' suggests that there is an attainable form of institution that is the university, and this we want to call into question. We have seen that many organizations call themselves universities: universities of the third age, corporate universities, people's universities, and so on. It is an ideological term that carries its own cultural connotations that need further examination.

Pelikan (1992, pp 12–13) in his re-examination of Newman's thesis, on the other hand, admits to the external social pressures and accuses the traditional universities of seeking to defend an untenable position:

> Through a deadly combination of internal confusion and external pressure, the university has all too often manoeuvred itself into a defence of the status quo, a carping posture in relation to the cultural and political mainstream, and a bunker mentality that can contribute to the widespread mentality for an attack.

Given that universities do not exist in splendid isolation from the pressures of the 'real' world, and that they are no longer ivory towers, we have shown in the previous chapters that Pelikan is not entirely correct. Universities have tried to respond to some of the social pressures of globalization, but with limited success. Their response has appeared to be almost unreflective, since they do not seem to know what the university is any longer. That is, they almost automatically respond to the pressures for social change. Even so, almost all of then have enunciated mission statements to tell whoever might read them what they believe their business to be about. But these statements read like short advertisements trying to convince a sceptical public that they are able to provide a quality service, and they are probably also treated by the public in a similar manner to the many other slogans that abound in this information age. Universities do need to know what they are, or at least what their mission is, so that they can respond to these external pressures in an appropriate manner, but mission statements differ from institution to institution – which actually implies that each university recognizes its own distinctive character and that we might really be discussing divergent rather than convergent forms of university. The university groupings, such as Universitas 21, also imply that universities are looking for similar partners in a diverse and fragmented world, and that they are already defining themselves as being different from other universities.

There is a sense in which we have acknowledged in this book that there might be common characteristics of the university or similar ideals as to what the university might be, and in Chapter 7 we used Barnett's characteristics of the university to assess the nature of the corporate universities; they are:

- critical interdisciplinarity;
- collective self-scrutiny;
- purposive renewal;
- moving borders;

- engagement;
- communicative tolerance.

We concluded that the corporate universities did not really fit into this characterization. Nevertheless these characteristics are themselves a mixture of an ideological statement about a perception of the university and a vision of the characteristics that these educational institutions might embrace. Another way of looking at them is to suggest that they are one person's route-map of the journey of being that those educational institutions perceived to be universities might take – although there is always the danger that they might lose their way, or get blown off course because of the many social pressures that are exerted on them to change direction. Consequently, they may probably never arrive at their destination, or because of the super-complex nature of contemporary society, only parts of the institution will remain true to the vision and keep on striving even though they might never arrive.

This chapter, consequently, has three main undertakings: first, to ask whether the term 'university' has meaning; second, to see if those institutions perceived to be universities actually have things in common and what, if anything, makes them different from other purveyors of learning materials; third, to highlight the fact that most discussion about the university might be perceived as discourse rather than either ontological or epistemological formulations, as Barnett (2000) suggests.

The concept of 'university'

It was relatively easy to provide meaning to the term 'university' when universities were defined in law or when the term was used only to refer to those educational institutions in the UK that had been granted a royal charter. Consequently, there was a tendency to assume that all universities were elite institutions, although it was always tacitly acknowledged that the elite institutions in France did not call themselves universities. However, the US system allowed a greater range of educational institutions to call themselves universities even though they were not all really elite institutions at all, but were educational organizations offering education beyond school. The elite then had to be differentiated from the remainder and were regarded as 'ivy league'; later other universities also attained elite recognition as a result of their achievements. No differentiation was made between further and higher education in the US system – all could call themselves universities. Conse-quently, when we read that the US universities are in crisis, as we have discussed throughout this book, it actually refers to a broader constituency of education than the universities in the British system – which are also in crisis.

Moreover, 'people's universities' have long existed in continental Europe: they are educational organizations that offer education to adults, as opposed to those that offered degree courses for young adults. The fact that some institutions conferred academic awards differentiated them from those other universities that did not. Following this continental tradition, therefore, when the universities of the third age were founded in France in 1972, they were also called universities. Now we also have corporate universities, and some of these are seeking to have their courses accredited. The exclusiveness of the term 'university' in the English language is being lost.

In the British system, and incidentally in the German one, the term implies a certain quality of education – higher rather than further – something that makes university education qualitatively different from other forms of education that occur after initial education. Its other use is merely with reference to forms of education that occur within a lifelong learning context. When Meister (1994) first wrote about the corporate universities, she called them 'corporate quality universities', although she removed the term 'quality' from the title of the second edition of her book, in 1998. Her use of the term, however, illustrates how the idea of quality can be associated with the concept and ideology of 'university', whatever the institution is and without demonstrating precisely what it is.

Since there is no intrinsic or legal meaning to the term, there is no way by which institutions can be prevented from calling themselves universities. Consequently, we need a framework by which we can compare them and through which we can locate them within the overall sector of society that might be termed post-school 'education'. In the discussion throughout this book the term 'university' is used to convey a variety of different forms of educational institution and four distinct dimensions have appeared in this discussion that enable us to characterize them, thus:

1. lifelong;
2. life wide;
3. level of qualification awarded;
4. function.

Dearing (1997), among other reports, has urged traditional universities to become institutions of lifelong education, although many of them have certainly not yet achieved this. Corporate universities would claim to offer lifelong education although they only offer a pattern of recurrent education to those who are in employment. Life wide education implies that all the types of knowledge discussed in Chapter 3 form the basis of the curriculum, but most institutions offer a curriculum of limited breadth – including many traditional universities. We have seen how corporate and private universities are seeking accreditation, and it would be possible to see this as a threefold categorization: non-award courses; certificates and diplomas to foundation (two-year) degree level; and bachelor's degree to higher doctorates. Finally, universities are usually seen to undertake three functions: research, which should include scholarship; teaching, which might also include consultancy; and service at local, national and international levels. Corporate universities have much more restricted functions and few appear to undertake research or scholarship, and service to the community is limited.

It will be noted that quality does not appear as a separate dimension in this framework, but that is because it should occur in all of the organization's functions and also in its administration. Quality pervades educational institutions, be it good or poor. We are aware that commodities do not always sell on the market because they are good – price and availability are other features that affect market performance. Nevertheless it is a feature of the market that purveyors of commodities and services often advertise that, for instance, they are members of professional and trade organizations in order to try to assure prospective customers that they offer a quality product or service. In precisely the same manner, many institutions might have adopted the term 'university' because it carries connotations of excellence.

Traditional universities are involved in their own quality and research assessment exercises and also in their own accreditation procedures – processes that have added to the stress of working in universities. But these processes also ensure that a level of quality is maintained and that the funding that they receive from government is well used. Nevertheless they are regulatory mechanisms, which also inhibit and hinder traditional universities from responding rapidly to the forces of change. But it might be argued that the production of quality products necessarily takes time, so that rapid response to market forces will push the quality downwards. At the same time, these mechanisms are valuable because they indicate that the universities are concerned about all forms of quality and that what they offer in the learning market is worthy of the quality implicit in the use of the term 'university'.

Traditional universities should make more of their own quality mechanisms, demonstrating that their products can be purchased with confidence, whether they are postgraduate teaching, residential programmes, short courses, consultancy practice or research. Obviously this suggestion moves the research and quality assessment exercises on from where they are at present, but both of them are designed to illustrate quality and in a competitive market these mechanisms can be reassuring to a general public that is continually hearing criticisms of universities for not offering the world of work the type of graduates that it wants.

The distinctive features of traditional universities

If we look briefly at the four dimensions of the university that we have suggested here, we can see that there are features that enable the traditional universities to be viewed as distinctive.

Lifelong

Few educational institutions offer programmes that are actually open to learners throughout the whole of their lives, or the whole of their lives from the time that they have completed their schooling – and in exceptional circumstances even during their schooling. Corporate universities, and the world of work, which have embraced the term 'lifelong learning' have done so as a rhetoric which they do not practice, since they offer no courses for people outside of work or for the elderly after they have finished their employment. Universities of the third age, as their name implies, only cater for those people who have retired, and so it is no more lifelong than that offered by the corporate universities. Traditional universities are moving towards implementing lifelong learning programmes while other universities, like the British Open University, actually do enable people of all ages to participate in their programmes.

Life wide

Traditional universities offer the broadest curricula of all the educational institutions, and it is possible to follow courses or research in most areas of knowledge. Universities of the third age allow for the possibility of a broad curriculum, although this does depend on the size of the university and its potential membership. By contrast, corporate universities offer narrow and specific curricula, but let it be emphasized that work–oriented learning is just as valuable to the human being as are the more liberal forms of education. Work is a necessity for people to survive in the contemporary global society and the learning processes do not change because of the nature of the education, so no attempt is made here to undermine the importance of these more specific curricula. What is perhaps most desirable is that curricula should be both wide and specific, catering for the needs or requirements of the learners and their sponsors.

Level of academic award

Traditional universities offer programmes that range from those that carry no award to those that enable doctorates to be earned. Universities have traditionally offered awards as evidence that the knowledge that they have taught has been learnt. No other educational institution calling itself a university has this range of academic accreditation, although we are increasingly seeing on the walls of shops and offices certificates that indicate that employees of the company have attended courses. The certificate is a symbol suggesting that the certificate holder is competent in the area for which the award has been made.

Functions

We have discussed the learning market throughout this book, and clearly all the institutions that call themselves universities offer learning opportunities: they all teach through one mode or another. By contrast, only some are engaged in research and it appears that even fewer value scholarship. Knowledge-intensive corporations tend to separate their research functions from their teaching ones, research remaining part of the company's functions, while the corporate universities are more orientated to didacticism. But scholarship seems unique to the traditional universities, even though it is fundamental to both teaching and research. Scholarship is something that universities need to re-emphasize far more since it is one of their functions that no other educational institution performs.

Service to local, regional, national and international communities is offered by the traditional universities, although it is not seen as important by all as it might be. Corporations also offer some service at all community levels, although this is not necessarily regarded as a function of corporate universities.

It may be seen that on all four dimensions that provide a framework by which we can analyse universities, the traditional universities are fundamentally different to the corporate universities. This does not mean that corporate universities cannot grow and develop in the way that traditional ones have done, nor does it mean that universities can rest on their laurels, since they do not all score highly on all four dimensions. In addition, this does not imply that these four functions are necessarily more valid descriptions of the 'university' than a list drawn up based on the characteristics of the corporate universities, when the traditional universities might be shown to undertake many superfluous functions.

The fifth dimension that all purveyors of commodities seek to demonstrate is that their products can be purchased with confidence since they are quality products manufactured under rigorous conditions. Traditional universities have their own quality assessment and quality control mechanisms in place, but there is a considerable need for research to see the extent to which other types of universities have similar mechanisms in place.

Frameworks such as this do not help define the university, but they do enable us to judge the different institutions that call themselves universities, and we can see some features of traditional universities that are unique to them. However, more empirical research needs to be undertaken into the nature of the corporate universities.

Discourse about the university

We have highlighted the fact that the concept 'university' does not actually relate to any one specific type of educational organization. We have also noted that Newman's idea that the end of the university is knowledge has fundamental difficulties as a result of the way that our understanding of knowledge has changed. Barnett (2000) tried to move the debate from epistemological to ontological issues, but he was still confronted with the fact that the term could not easily be defined in a way that would allow it to make sense of the multifarious manifestations of universities in contemporary society. Consequently, it is now not what the term actually means that is important, but what it is perceived to mean in relation to the wider world; the result of the discourse is significant.

Discourses are statements that provide a language for discussing institutions and phenomena; that is, they represent these phenomena in certain ways. But, as Foucault pointed out (Sheridan, 1980, p 123), individuals have a propensity to believe what they are told, that is, to believe the content of the discourse, and so it is vitally important to those who hold power to control the discourse about social phenomena in general. The traditional universities do need to demonstrate that they really do control this discourse about the university and that they can define its meaning in contemporary society.

Hence emphasis has been placed on criticality in a great deal of writing, not only about the nature of university education, but also about the education of adults in general. Barnett (1997) for instance, focused on this as a central feature of his understanding of higher education, although we would argue here that it should be central to all education, and that learners can be encouraged to unpack whatever truth the discourses they examine might contain. In a sense, this is precisely what we have been doing here.

In Newman's day, knowledge was closely related to truth and so it could be claimed that when he argued that the end of the university is knowledge, he might actually have been arguing that universities were institutions which endeavoured to understand the truth about the universe and then to disseminate the knowledge that had been discovered. Universities are, therefore, about humanity's desire to discover truth rather than about truth itself. This means that they exist to discover truth in every walk of life and in all aspects of the universe. Their methods should still remain rigorous and scientific, in the broadest sense of that word, but what they discover may only be relative, for knowledge changes at different speeds, as Scheler ([1926] 1980) demonstrated.

For Foucault, the truth is to be found in the discourse that relates its meaning to the world. This is the function of the educational system according to him, and it is this that we have analysed, in part, in this book. But as Lukes (1974) has also shown, there are some who have the power to define the discourse and either to get it on to or to get it removed from the agenda of contemporary society, while others do not have such power. And, as we pointed out in Chapter 2, power lies with those who control the global substructure – capital in all its forms, and information technology. It is they who have the power to define the discourse about the university in the future and to get their discourse about the university on to the educational agenda. They also control the corporate universities.

We are already seen in this book that those who hold this power are beginning to:

- define the discourses about education as being a preparation for work rather than a preparation for life;
- define lifelong education in terms of work life education;
- influence the direction that academic research might take;
- define citizenship in terms of employability and being a member of a corporation, rather than in terms of duties and obligations of service to society, and so on.

There is a danger, therefore, that if the corporate universities continue to expand at their present rate, they will also influence the discourse about the nature of the university, even though they offer only a specialized and restricted curriculum. Indeed, they might eventually dominate it to such an extent that the traditional universities are portrayed as providing many programmes and courses and undertaking research projects that are irrelevant to the world of the global capitalist market. They might then be portrayed as irrelevant themselves. If this discourse is believed, then universities might be forced to curtail their curricula in order to make them appear relevant to these concerns, especially if government funding is also targeted in the same direction.

There is no place in this argument for conspiracy-type theories – it is merely the way that the global capitalist system operates, utilizing a form of instrumental rationality. We assume the correctness of instrumental rationality, even though it is merely another discourse. There are other forms of rationality, such as value rationality, but they are dominated by the taken-for-granted instrumental rationality of modernity and so the danger exists that the discourse about the nature of the university will be dominated by such instrumentally rational discourses. Since the traditional universities seem not to know precisely what they are, it is even easier for such an instrumentally rational discourse to become believed and dominant and, in a sense, this is part of what we have been exploring throughout this book.

Conclusion

So what is the university? What is it that is in crisis? Simple questions to pose, but difficult ones to answer!

Following Foucault's analysis, the university is a part of the social institution that seeks to respond to humanity's will to understand the truth in every walk of life and in the universe within which all human life is lived. Its understanding might well be less than complete and almost totally relative, but this is the paradox of meaning – every discovery reveals more things that remain unknown; new discoveries might also contradict old ones and so on. The process of seeking to understand is never-ending. But the will to truth demands an educational institution that offers, as a service to everybody who wishes to participate, lifelong and life wide quality research, scholarship and teaching. The academic qualification is less relevant than the learning itself. But this is a discourse about the university that it needs to espouse and one that universities need to keep on publicizing in the face of alternative discourses and the social forces that continue to pressurize them; it is also what the universities should aspire to be.

References

Ahrens University (nd) *Ahrens University* www.ahrensuniversity.com/

Albrow, M and King, E (eds) (1990) *Globalization, Knowledge and Society*, Sage, London

Althusser, L (1973) 'Ideology and ideological state apparatus', in B R Cosin, *Education, Structure and Society*, Penguin, Harmondsworth

Amit, V (2000) 'The university as panopticon', in M Strathern (ed) *Audit Cultures – Anthropological studies in accountability, ethics and the academy*, Routledge, London

Apps, J (1989) 'Providers of adult and continuing education: A framework', in S Merriam and P Cunningham (eds) *Handbook of Adult and Continuing Education*, Jossey-Bass, San Francisco

Archer, M (1990) 'Theory, culture and post-industrial society', in M Featherstone (ed) *Global Culture*, Sage, London

Aristotle (1925 edn) *The Nicomachean Ethics*, trans D Ross, Oxford University Press, Oxford

Aronovitz, S (2000) *The Knowledge Factory – Dismantling the corporate university and creating true higher learning*, Beacon Press, Boston

Ball, C (1992) *Profitable Learning*, Royal Society of Arts, London

Barnett, R (1990) *The Idea of Higher Education*, Open University Press, Buckingham, in association with the Society for Research into Higher Education

Barnett, R (1994) *The Limits of Competence*, Open University Press, Buckingham, in association with the Society for Research into Higher Education

Barnett, R (1997) *Higher Education: A Critical Business*, Open University Press, Buckingham, in association with the Society for Research into Higher Education

Barnett, R (2000) *Realizing the University*, Open University Press, Buckingham, in association with the Society for Research into Higher Education

Baron, S, Stalker, K, Wilkinson, H and Riddell, S (1998) 'The learning society. The highest stage of human capitalism?', in F Coffield (ed) *Learning at Work*, Policy Press, Bristol

Baskett, M and Marsick, V (eds) (1992) *Professionals' Ways of Knowing: New findings on how to improve professional education*, Jossey-Bass, San Francisco

Baudrillard, J (1988) 'The system of objects', in M Poster (ed) *Jean Baudrillard: Selected Writings*, Polity Press, Cambridge

Bauman, Z (1987) *Legislators and Interpreters*, Polity Press, Cambridge

Bauman, Z (1992) *Intimations of Postmodernity*, Routledge, London

Bauman, Z (1995) *Life in Fragments*, Blackwell, Oxford

Bauman, Z (1998a) *Globalization: the Human Consequences*, Polity Press, Cambridge

Bauman, Z (1998b) *Work, Consumerism and the New Poor*, Open University Press, Buckingham

Bauman, Z (1999) *In Search of Politics*, Polity Press, Cambridge

Beck, U (1992) *The Risk Society*, Sage, London

Beck, U (1994) 'The reinvention of politics', in U Beck, A Giddens and S Lash (eds) *Reflexive Modernization*, Polity Press, Cambridge

Beck, U (2000) *What is Globalization?*, Polity Press, Cambridge

Beck, U, Giddens, A and Lash, S (eds) (1994) *Reflexive Modernization*, Polity Press, Cambridge

Beinart, S and Smith, P (1997) *National Learning Survey*, Research Report No 49, Department for Education and Employment, London

Belenky, M F, Clinchy, B M, Goldberger, N R and Tarule, J M (1986) *Women's Ways of Knowing*, Basic Books, New York

Bell, D (1973) *The Coming of Post-Industrial Society*, Basic Books, New York

Blight, D, Davis, D and Olsen, A (2000) 'The globalization of higher education', in P Scott (ed) *Higher Education Re-formed*, Falmer, London

Blustain, H, Goldstein, P and Lozier, G (1999) 'Assessing the new competitive landscape', in R Katz and Associates *Dancing with the Devil*, Jossey-Bass, San Francisco

Borger, R and Seaborne, A (1966) *The Psychology of Learning*, Penguin, Harmondsworth

Bornschier, V (1980) 'Multinational corporations and economic growth', *Journal of Development Economics*, **7**, pp 191–210

Boud, D (ed) (1985) *Problem-Based Learning in Education for the Professions*, Higher Education Research and Development Society of Australasia, Sydney

Boud, D, Keogh, R and Walker, D (1985) *Reflection: Turning experience into learning*, Croom Helm, Beckenham

Boud, D and Feletti, G (eds) (1991) *The Challenge of Problem Based Learning*, Kogan Page, London

Bourdieu, P (1973) 'Cultural reproduction and social reproduction', in R Brown (ed) *Knowledge, Education and Social Change*, Tavistock, London

Bourdieu, P (1984) *Distinction: A social critique of the judgement of taste*, Routledge and Kegan Paul, London

Bourdieu, P (1990) *The Logic of Practice,* Polity Press, Cambridge

Bourgeois, E, Duke, C, Luc-Guyot, J and Merrill, B (1999) *The Adult University,* Open University Press, Buckingham, in association with the Society for Research into Higher Education

Bowles, S and Gintis, H (1976) *Schooling in Capitalist America,* Routledge and Kegan Paul, London

Brandon, P (1999) 'Salford University: An historical industrial partnership', in H Gray (ed) *Universities and the Creation of Wealth*, SRHE and Open University, Buckingham

Brown, G and Atkins, M (1988) *Effective Teaching in Higher Education,* Methuen, London

Cabal, A B (1993) *The University as an Institution Today,* UNESCO, Paris

Campbell, C (1987) *The Romantic Ethic and the Spirit of Modern Consumerism,* Blackwell, Oxford

Campbell, D (1984) *The New Majority,* University of Alberta Press, Edmonton

Carlson, R (1987) *The Americanization Syndrome,* Croom Helm, Beckenham

Carnevale, A, Gainer, L and Villet, J (1990a) *Training in America,* Jossey Bass, San Francisco

Carnevale, A, Gainer, L and Villet, J (1990b) *Training the Technical Work Force,* Jossey-Bass, San Francisco

Casner-Lotto, J and Associates (1988) *Successful Training Strategies,* Jossey-Bass, San Francisco

Caspar, P (1992) 'France', in P Jarvis (ed)

Castells, M (1996) *The Rise of the Network Society,* Vol 1 of *The Information Age: Economy, Society and Culture,* Blackwell, Oxford

Cattell, R (1943) 'The measurement of adult intelligence', *Psychological Bulletin,* pp 153–93

Chase, N (1998) 'Lessons from the corporate university', *Quality Magazine,* June, www.quality,ag.com/articles/1998/jun98/0698tt.html

Coffield, F (ed) (2000) *Differing Visions of the Learning Society,* Policy Press, Bristol and ESRC (Vol 1)

Coleman, J (1990) *Foundations of Social Theory,* Belknap Press, Harvard

Collomb, B and Seidal, H (1998) 'Foreword', in L Otala *European Approaches to Lifelong Learning,* European University-Industry Forum, Geneva

Crainer, S (WWW) 'Corporate views of university', *Management Skills and Development Magazine,* www.managementskills.co.uk/articles/univer.htm

Crossley, B (1976) 'The future of higher or university adult education in Britain and the USA', *Comparative Education,* March, cited by A Thornton and M Stephens (eds) (1977) *The University in its Region*, Department of Adult Education, University of Nottingham, Nottingham

CVCP/HEFCE (2000) *The Business of Borderless Education: Summary Report,* CVCP, London

Daniel, J (1996) *Mega-Universities and Knowledge Media,* Kogan Page, London

Dearing, R (chair) (1997) *Higher Education in the Learning Society: Summary report,* HM Government, London

Delors, J (Chair) (1996) *Learning the Treasure Within,* UNESCO, Paris

Department for Education and Employment (1997) *National Learning Survey,* Research Report No 49, DfEE, London

Department for Education and Employment (DfEE) (1998a) *The Learning Age,* DfEE, London

DfEE (1998b) *Further Education for the New Millennium,* DfEE, London

DfEE (1998c) *Learning Towns, Learning Cities,* DfEE, London

DeSai Systems (1999) *Corporate University Benefits and Features* (www.c. university.com/cu_benefits_features/cu_benefits_features.htm)

Duderstadt, J (1999) 'Can colleges and universities survive in the information age?', in R Katz and Associates *Dancing with the Devil,* Jossey-Bass, San Francisco

Duke, C (1992) *The Learning University,* Open University Press, Buckingham, in association with the Society for Research into Higher Education

Durkheim, E ([1893] 1933) *The Division of Labor in Society,* Basic Books, New York

Durkheim, E (1956) *Education and Sociology,* Free Press, New York

ePath Learning *Getting Started with BuildKit* www.epathlearning.com/ new_user/index.html

Eraut, M (1997) 'Perspectives of defining the "Learning Society"', *Journal of Education Policy,* **12**, 6, pp 551–58

Eurich, N (1985) *Corporate Classrooms,* Carnegie Foundation for the Advancement of Teaching, Princeton

Eurich, N (1990) *The Learning Industry,* Carnegie Foundation for the Advancement of Teaching, Princeton

European Union (1995) *Teaching and Learning: Towards the learning society,* European Union, Brussels

European Union (2000) *Towards a European Research Area,* Communication from the Commission to the Council, the European Parliament, the Economic and Social Committee and the Committee of the Regions, Brussels

Farringdon, G (1999) 'The new technologies and the future of residential undergraduate education', in R Katz and Associates *Dancing with the Devil,* Jossey-Bass, San Francisco

Featherstone, L (2000) 'The new student movement: Protests rock the corporate university', *Nation Magazine,* 15 May (www.thirdworldtraveler. com/Youth/NewStudentMovement.htlm)

Featherstone, M (1991) *Consumer Culture and Postmodernism,* Sage, London

Featherstone, M (ed) (1990) *Global Culture,* Sage, London

Featherstone, M, Lash, S and Robertson, R (eds) (1995) *Global Modernities,* Sage, London

Feigenbaum, E and McCorduck, P (1984) *The Fifth Generation,* Signet, New York

Flew, A (1976) *A Dictionary of Philosophy,* Pan Books, London

Foucault, M (1972) *The Archaeology of Knowledge,* Routledge, London

Frenkel, S, Korczynski, M, Shire, K and Tam, M (1999) *On the Front Line,* Cornell University Press, Ithaca

Friedman, J (1994) *Cultural Identity and Global Process,* Sage, London

Fukuyama, F (1995) *Trust: The social virtues and the creation of prosperity,* Penguin, Harmondsworth

Galtung, I (1971) 'A structural theory of imperialism', *Journal of Peace Studies,* **8**, pp 81–117

Gibbons, M *et al* (ed) (1994) *The New Production of Knowledge,* Sage, London

Giddens, A (1990) *The Consequence of Modernity,* Polity Press, Cambridge

Giddens, A (1998) *The Third Way,* Polity Press, Cambridge

Goddard, A (2000a) 'Unpaid slog sustains research', *Times Higher Education Supplement,* 12 May, p 1

Goddard, A (2000b) 'Universitas 21 deal for online MBA', *Times Higher Education Supplement,* 24 November, p 16

Goddard, J (1999) 'How universities can thrive locally in a global economy', in H Gray (ed) *Universities and the Creation of Wealth,* SRHE and Open University, Buckingham

Gouldner, A W (1957-58) 'Cosmopolitans and locals: Towards an analysis of latent social roles', *Administrative Science Quarterly,* **2**, 1–2

Gray, H (ed) (1999) *Universities and the Creation of Wealth,* SRHE and Open University Press, Buckingham

Greenhaigh, T and Maslen, G (2000) 'Media deal is future for U21', *Times Higher Education Supplement,* 19 May, p 13

Griffin, C (1999) 'Lifelong learning and welfare reform', *The International Journal of Lifelong Education,* **18**, 6, pp 431–52

Griffith, W (1980) 'Coordination of personnel, programs and services', in J Peters and Associates *Building an Effective Adult Education Enterprise,* Jossey-Bass, San Francisco

Groombridge, B (1972) *Television and the People,* Penguin, Harmondsworth

Habermas, J (1972) *Knowledge and Human Interests,* Heinemann, Oxford

Hamilton, P (1992) 'The enlightenment and the birth of social science', in S Hall and B Gieben (eds) *Formations of Modernity,* Polity Press, Cambridge, in association with the Open University

Harvey, D (1990) *The Condition of Postmodernity,* Blackwell, Oxford

Held, D (1992) 'The development of the modern university', in S Hall and B Gieben (eds) *Formations of Modernity,* Polity Press, Cambridge, in association with the Open University

Heller, A (1984) *Everyday Knowledge,* Routledge and Kegan Paul, London

Houle, C (1961) *The Enquiring Mind,* University of Wisconsin Press, Wisconsin

Houle, C (1980) *Continuing Learning in the Professions,* Jossey-Bass, San Francisco

Husen, T (1974) *The Learning Society,* Methuen, London

Hutchins, R M (1968) *The Learning Society,* Penguin, Harmondsworth

Illich, I and Verne, E (1976) *Imprisoned in the Global Classroom,* Writers and Readers Publishing, London

James, W ([1907] 1995) *Pragmatism,* Dover Publications, New York

Jarvis, P (1977) 'Protestant Ministers: Job satisfaction and role strain in the bureaucratic organisation of the church', University of Aston, unpublished PhD thesis

Jarvis, P (1987) *Adult Learning in the Social Context,* Croom Helm, Beckenham

Jarvis, P (ed) (1992) *Paradoxes of Learning,* Jossey-Bass, San Francisco

Jarvis, P (1995) *Adult and Continuing Education: Theory and practice,* 2nd edn, Routledge, London

Jarvis, P (1995a) 'Educating the adult educator in an information society: The role of the university', in M Collins (ed) *The Canmore Proceedings,* University of Saskatchewan, Saskatchewan, pp 179–88

Jarvis, P (1996) 'The public recognition of lifetime learning', *Lifelong Learning in Europe,* **196,** pp 10–17

Jarvis, P (1999) *The Practitioner Researcher: Developing Theory from Practice,* Jossey-Bass, San Francisco

Jarvis, P (2000) 'Globalisation, the learning society and comparative education', *Comparative Education,* **36,** 3, pp 343–55

Jarvis, P (2001a) *Learning in Later Life,* Kogan Page, London

Jarvis, P (2001b) 'Globalisation, citizenship and the education of adults in contemporary society' *Compare* (forthcoming – BAICE President's Address)

Jarvis, P (ed) (1992) *Perspectives on Adult Education and Training in Europe,* NIACE, Leicester

Jarvis, P, Holford, J and Griffin, C (1998) *Theory and Practice of Learning,* Kogan Page, London

Jarvis, P, Holford, J, Griffin, C and Dubelaar, J (1997) *Towards the Learning City,* Corporation of London Education Department, London

Jones International University (1999) *Academics Accreditation* www.jones international.edu/academics/accreditation/index.html

Kant, I (1934 edn) *Critique of Pure Reason,* Everyman, London

Katz, R (1999) 'Competitive strategies for higher education in the information age', in R Katz and Associates *Dancing with the Devil*, Jossey-Bass, San Francisco

Katz, R and Associates (1999) *Dancing with the Devil*, Jossey-Bass, San Francisco

Kenny-Wallace, G (2000) 'Plato.com: The role and impact of corporate universities in the third millennium', in P Scott (ed) *Higher Education Reformed*, Falmer, London

Kerr, C, Dunlop, J, Harbison, F and Myers, C (1973) *Industrialism and Industrial Man,* 2nd edn, Penguin, Harmondsworth

Kett, J F (1994) *The Pursuit of Useful Knowledge under Difficulties,* Stanford University Press, Stanford

Kinman, G (2000) 'Would you choose your job again?', *Times Higher Education Supplement,* 14 April, p 18

Knapper, C and Cropley, A (1985) *Lifelong Learning and Higher Education,* Croom Helm, Beckenham

Knowles, M (1980) 'The growth and development of adult education', in J Peter and Associates *Building an Effective Adult Education Enterprise,* Jossey-Bass, San Francisco

Knowles, M (1991) 'Epilogue' in J Peters and P Jarvis *Adult Education: Evolution and achievements in a developing field of study,* Jossey-Bass, San Francisco

Kolb, D (1984) *Experiential Learning,* Prentice Hall, Englewood Cliffs, NJ

Korton, D (1995) *When Corporations Rule the World,* Earthscan, London

Kuosmanen, R (Chair) (1999) *Adult Education Policy in the First Years of the 21st Century,* Adult Education Council, Helsinki

Kwan, C-Y (2000) 'Problem-based learning in medical education: From McMaster to Asia-Pacific Region' in *TLHE Symposium* (eds) C Wang, K P Mohaanan, D Pan and Y S Chee

Learmonth, J assisted by Maidment, L (eds) (1993) *Teaching and Learning in Cities,* Whitbread Educational Partnership, Luton

Learn University (www.learnu.com/noflash.html)

Levine, A and Associates (1990) *Shaping Higher Education's Future,* Jossey-Bass, San Francisco

Lewis, C (1996) *Crisis in the Academy,* Macmillan, London

Lohman, D and Scheurman, G (1992) 'Fluid abilities and epistemic thinking: Some prescriptions for adult education', in A Tijnman and M van der Kamp (eds) *Learning Across the Lifespan*, Pergamon, Oxford

Long, H (1983) *Adult Learning,* Cambridge Press, New York

Long, H and Associates (1998) *Developing Paradigms for Self-Directed Learning,* College of Education, University of Oklahoma, Norman, OK

Longworth, N and Davies, W K (1996) *Lifelong Learning,* Kogan Page, London

Lucas, C J (1996) *Crisis in the Academy,* Macmillan, London

LucentTechnologies (1996) *Distance Learning – the Vision,* LucentTechnologies Center for Excellence in Distance Education (www.lucent.com/cedl/)

Lukes, S (1974) *Power: A radical view,* Macmillan, London

Lyotard, J-F (1984) *The Post-Modern Condition: A report on knowledge,* Manchester University Press, Manchester

Lyotard, J-F (1992) *The Postmodern Explained to Children,* Turnaround, London

Marsick, V and Watkins, K (1990) *Informal and Incidental Learning in the Workplace,* Routledge, London

McDonalds (nd) *Hamburger University* www.mcdonalds.com/corporate/careers/hambuniv/hambuniv.html

McGivney, V (1999) *Informal Learning in the Community,* NIACE, Leicester

McInerney, C and LeFerve, D (2000) 'Knowledge managers', in C Prichard *et al* (eds) *Managing Knowledge,* Macmillan Business, London

McNiff, J (1988) *Action Research: Principles ands practice,* Macmillan, London

Megginson, D and Clutterbuck, D (1995) *Mentoring in Action,* Kogan Page, London

Meister, J (1994) *Corporate Quality Universities,* Irwin, Burr Ridge, Ill, and the American Society for Training and Development

Meister, J (1998) *Corporate Universities* (revised and updated edition) McGraw-Hill, New York

Mercer, L (1998) *The Stanford Daily online* (daily.Stanford.org/daily97-98/5-27-98/NEWS/SCIcorporate27.html)

Merton, R K (1968) *Social Theory and Social Structure* (enlarged edn) Free Press, New York

Ministry of Education (1999) *Information, Training and Research in the Information Society: A national strategy for 2000–2004,* Ministry of Education, Helsinki

Monbiot, G (2000) 'Getting into bed with big business', *The Guardian,* 31 August

Motorola.com (nd) *About Motorola University* mu.motorola.com/About MU.html

Newman, J H (1976 edn) *The Idea of the University Defined and Illustrated,* Clarendon, Oxford

Newson, J (1998) 'The corporate-linked university: From social product to market force', *Canadian Journal of Communications,* **23**, 1 (www.wlu.ca/wwwpress/jrls/cjc/BackIssues/13.1/newson.htlm)

Niebuhr, H Jr (1984) *Revitalizing American Learning,* Wadsworth, Belmont

NoonTime University noontimeu.com/

Nozick, R (1974) *Anarchy, State and Utopia,* Blackwell, Oxford

Nyiri, J (1988) 'Tradition and practical knowledge', in J Nyiri and B Smith (eds) *Practical Knowledge,* Croom Helm, Beckenham

Nyiri, J and Smith, B (eds) (1988) *Practical Knowledge,* Croom Helm, Beckenham

Organisation for Economic Cooperation and Development (1996) *Lifelong Learning for All,* OECD, Paris

Otala, L (1998) *European Approaches to Lifelong Learning,* European University-Industry Forum, Geneva

Passat, R (1997) 'Ces promesses des technologies de l'immaterial', *Le Monde Diplomatique,* July, p 26

Pedlar, M, Burgoyne, J and Boydell, T (1996) *The Learning Company,* 2nd edn, McGraw-Hill, Maidenhead

Pelikan, J (1992) *The Idea of the University: A re-examination,* Yale University Press, New Haven

Peters, J and Associates (1980) *Building an Effective Adult Education Enterprise,* Jossey-Bass, San Francisco

Peters, J, Jarvis, P and Associates (1991) *Adult Education: Evolution and achievements in a developing field of study,* Jossey-Bass, San Francisco

Peters, O (1984) 'Distance education and industrial production: A comparative interpretation in outline', in D Seward *et al* (eds) *Distance Education: International perspectives,* Routledge, London

Phillips, D (1986) *Toward a Just Social Order,* Princeton University Press, Princeton, NJ

Piaget, J (1929) *The Child's Conception of the World,* Routledge and Kegan Paul, London

Polanyi, M (1967) *The Tacit Dimension,* Routledge and Kegan Paul, London

Poster, M (ed) (1988) *Jean Baudrillard: Selected writings,* Polity Press, Cambridge

Powell, L E (1993) 'Fostering excellence and equity in education: The role of the school system', in J Learmonth (ed) *Teaching and Learning in Cities,* Whitbread Educational Partnership, Luton

Preece, J (1999) *Using Foucault and Feminist Theory to Explain Why Some Adults are Excluded from British University Education,* Edwin Mellon, Lampeter

Prichard, C, Hull, R, Chumer, M and Willmott, H (eds) (2000) *Managing Knowledge,* Macmillan Business, London

Putnam, R (1996) 'Who killed civic America?', *Prospect,* March, pp 66–72

Quality Magazine (1998) 'Lessons from the corporate university', June, www.qqualitymag.com/articles/1998/jun98/0698tt.html

Ranson, S (1994) *Towards the Learning Society,* Cassell, London

Rastel, E (1998) *The McKinsey Way,* McGraw-Hill, New York

Rawls, J (1971) *A Theory of Justice,* The Belknap Press of Harvard University Press, Cambridge, MA

Reich, R (1991) *The Work of Nations,* Simon & Schuster, London

Rifkin, J (1995) *The End of Work,* G P Putnam's Sons, New York

Ritzer, G (1993) *The McDonaldization of Society,* Pine Forge Press, Thousand Oaks

Robertson, R (1992) *Globalization,* Sage, London

Robertson, R (1995) 'Glocalization', in M Featherstone *et al* (eds) *Global Modernities,* Sage, London

Rogers, C (1969) *Freedom to Learn* (subsequent edns 1983, 1994) Merrill, Columbus, OH

Rowley, D, Lujan, H and Dolence, M (1998) *Strategic Choices for the Academy,* Jossey-Bass, San Francisco

Rumble, G and Harry, K (eds) (1982) *The Distance Teaching Universities,* Croom Helm, Beckenham

Russell, L (chair) (1973) *Adult Education: A plan for development,* The Stationery Office, Norwich

Scheffler, I (1965) *Conditions of Knowledge,* University of Chicago Press, Chicago, IL

Scheler, M ([1926] 1980) *Problems of a Sociology of Knowledge,* Routledge and Kegan Paul, London

Schon, D (1983) *The Reflective Practitioner,* Basic Books, New York

Schon, D (1987) *Educating the Reflective Practitioner,* Jossey-Bass, San Francisco

Schugurensky, D (nd) McDonald's starts first corporate university, fcis.oise. utontario.ca/~daniel_schugurensky/assignment/1961mcdonalds. html

Schuler, T (1997) 'Relations between human and social capital', in F Coffield (ed) *A National Strategy for Lifelong Learning,* University of Newcastle Dept of Education, Newcastle

Schumpeter, J (1976) *Capitalism, Socialism and Democracy,* George Allen and Unwin, London

Schutte, F and van der Sijde, P (eds) (2000) *The University and its Region,* Twente University Press, Enschede

Scott, P (1984) *The Crisis of the University,* Croom Helm, Beckenham

Scott, P (ed) (1998) *The Globalization of Higher Education,* Open University Press, Buckingham, in association with the Society for Research into Higher Education

Scott, P (ed) (2000) *Higher Education Re-formed,* Falmer, London

Seabrook, J (1988) *The Race for Riches: The human cost of wealth,* Marshall Pickering, Basingstoke

Senge, P (1990) *The Fifth Discipline,* Doubleday, New York

Seville, A and Tooley, J (1997) *The Debate on Higher Education,* Institute of Economic Affairs Education and Training Unit, London

Seward, D, Keegan, D and Holmberg, B (eds) (1984) *Distance Education: International perspectives,* Routledge, London

Shattock, M (2000) 'The impact of a new university on its region', in F Schutte and P van der Sijde (eds) *The University and its Regions,* Twente University Press, Enschede

Sheridan, A (1980) *Michael Foucault: The will to truth,* Tavistock, London

Short, D and Jarvis, P (2000) 'Developing workplace leaders through their emotional reactions', unpublished paper presented at the Academy of Human Resource Development North Carolina, USA, March

Shumar, W (1997) *College for Sale,* Falmer, London

Sinnott, J and Johnson, L (1996) *Reinventing the University,* Ablex, Norwood, NJ

Sobol, T (1993) 'Introduction', in J Learmonth (ed) *Teaching and Learning in Cities,* Whitbread Educational Partnership, Luton

SRI (nd) *Organizational Development and Training – Corporate university development* www.sri.com/policy/orgdev/univ.html

Stehr, N (1994) *Knowledge Societies,* Sage, London

Strathern, M (ed) (2000) *Audit Cultures – Anthropological studies in accountability, ethics and the academy,* Routledge, London

Stromquist, N and Samoff, J (2000) 'Knowledge management systems', *Compare,* **30**, 3, pp 323–32

Swieringa, J and Wierdsma, A (1992) *Becoming a Learning Organization: Beyond the learning curve,* Addison–Wesley, Wokingham

Targett, S (1999) 'Traditional institutions are alarmed by the rise of private academies providing company-specific courses and research', *Financial Times,* 20 January

Thornton, A and Stephens, M (eds) (1977) *The University in its Region,* Department of Adult Education, University of Nottingham, Nottingham

Thompson, P, Warhurst, C and Callaghan (2000) 'Human capital or capitalising on humanity?', in C Prichard *et al* (eds) *Managing Knowledge,* Macmillan Business, London

Tight, M (1991) *Higher Education: A part-time perspective,* Open University Press, Buckingham, in association with the Society for Research into Higher Education

Tijnman, A and van der Kamp, M (eds) (1992) *Learning Across the Lifespan,* Pergamon, Oxford

Times Higher Education Supplement (1999) 'Corporate unis muscle in', 9 July, p 3

Tooley, J (1996) *Education without the State,* Institute of Economic Affairs Education and Training Unit, London

Tough, A (1972) *The Adult's Learning Projects,* 2nd edn, Ontario Institute for Studies in Education, Toronto

Tuomi, I (1999) *Corporate Knowledge,* Metaxis, Helsinki

UNESCO (1998) *Summary of the World Declaration on Higher Education for the Twenty First Century,* UNESCO, Paris

Wallersten, I (1974) *The Modern World System,* Academic Press, New York

Walt Disney World (nd) *Alumni Association of Cornell University* www.rso. cornell.edu/disney/

Warren, D (1991) 'What is indigenous knowledge?', from www.worldbank. org/afr/ik/basic.htm

Watkins, K and Marsick, V (1993) *Sculpting the Learning Organization,* Jossey-Bass, San Francisco

Weber, M (1947) 'Class, status, party', in H H Gerth and C W Mills (eds) *From Max Weber,* Routledge and Kegan Paul, London

Weber, M (1971) *The Protestant Ethic and the Spirit of Capitalism,* Unwin University Books, London

Weede, E (1990) 'Rent seeking or dependency as explanations of why poor people stay poor', in M Albrow and E King (eds) *Globalization, Knowledge and Society,* Sage, London

Weil, S and McGill, I (1989) *Making Sense of Experiential Learning,* Open University Press, Buckingham in association with the Society for Research into Higher Education

White, S (2000) *Corporate University,* www.houstonisd.org/achievemeentinst/ aileadership/corporateuniversities.htm

Willis, S and Dubin, S (eds) (1990) *Maintaining Professional Competence,* Jossey-Bass, San Francisco

Wilkerson, L and Hundert, E (1991) 'Becoming a problem-based tutor: Increasing self-awareness through faculty development', in D Boud and G Feletti (eds) *The Challenge of Problem Based Learning,* Kogan Page, London

Young, M (1998) *The Curriculum for the Future,* Falmer, London

Index

Page references in italics indicate figures or tables.

academic awards   146
academic staff   2, 58
   and accreditation   8
   bureaucratic role   99
   changing role   17–18, *18*, 61
   dissemination of knowledge
      58–59
   and globalization   25–26
   intellectual copyright   59
   and learning market   10–11
   and learning materials   16
   and research   50, 52, 102
   service role   35
   training   103–04, 104–05
accreditation   146
   corporate universities   114–15
   prior learning   8, 69
administration   97–100, 124
adult education   125, 130–01
Ahrens University   122
artificial knowledge   13, 43
assessment systems   7, 71

Barnett, R   123, 123–24, 126, 140
British Open University   15, 72,
   86

Canada   51

capitalism   4, 5–6, 21, 22, 24, 39,
   57
Church, the   3–4
cities, learning   88–91
citizenship   29, 84, 119–20
Coach U   117
commercialization of research
   51–52, 101–02
community colleges, USA   126,
   127
community service   34–5, 89–91
computers   38
consultancy   40, 122, 133, 134,
   138
consumerism   86
content knowledge   48, 50
copyright   59
corporate ethos and universities
   96–97, 107–10
   administration and structure
      97–100
   pedagogic activities   100–01
   research   101–02
corporate universities   6, 93–4,
   104, 111–12, 128
   characteristics and programmes
      116–22
   history and expansion   112–16

and learning industry   132–34
as universities   122–28
within universities   103–04,
    104–06
corporations   22–23, 29, 97
citizenship   119–20
and globalization   21
grants   9
in-house education   112–13
knowledge management   53–5
learning organizations   92,
    93–94
and research   15, 50–51, 51–52

Dearing Report (1977)   30–31,
    81–82, 103
developing countries   24, 28
discourse   44, 68, 147–48
disjuncture   47, 65, 74
distance education   8–9, 15–16,
    72–74, 117
doctorates   7

e-universities   72
economic globalization *see*
    globalization
education   5, 25
as a commodity   8–9
and learning   65–66
and work   30–31
empirical knowledge   4, 11, 41, 75
employability   5, 84
employment   39, 40, 83
engagement   125
Enlightenment, the   4, 44
ePath Learning   134
epistemological restructuring   125
epistemology   12, 40
ethical issues   28–29, 52
experience   41, 49, 62, 64, 92–93
tacit dimension   47, 48

experimentation   41
extramural courses   136

fees   8
Finland   30
folk knowledge   45–46
Foucault, M   43–44
funding   8, 9, 31–32
research   14, 51, 52

globality   21
globalization   20–25, 35–36, 79,
    93
and knowledge   43, 44, 56
opportunities   25–27
problems   27–29
glocalization   33, 43, 44
government *see* state, the
grants   9

habitualization   47, 65, 93
Hamburger University, USA   112
higher education   1, 5, 25
and adult education   131
funding   31–32
and work   30–31
see also universities
Hong Kong   90

Iams Company   114
independent knowledge   13
indigenous knowledge (IK)
    45–46
inequality   24, 28
information   38
information technology   21,
    21–22, 37, 39
and distance education   60, 72,
    73
intellectual capital   22, 37, 39, 40,
    53

intellectual copyright   59
intellectuals
   political power   5
   see also academic staff
interdisciplinarity, critical   124
Internet   16, 73–74, 134, 138–39

knowledge   4, 37, 57–58, 87
   changing forms   11–13, 22, 42
   as a commodity   9
   dissemination   58–60
   and experience   62
   managing   53–55
   nature of   22, 40–6
   practical   46–50, *49*, 70–71
   and research   50–53
knowledge societies   6, 9, 37, 57
   nature of   38–40
knowledge workers   6, 7, 39, 53

Land–Grant Colleges, USA   12
Learn University   117
learners   63–64, 119
learning   58, 61–65, *64*, 67, 78,
   129
   corporate universities   119
   and education   65–66
   innovations in teaching   69–71
   and research   74–76
learning cities   88–91
learning industry   129–31, 138–39
   corporate universities   132–34
   universities   135–38, 139
   see also lifelong learning
learning market   8–11, 86–88
learning materials   16, 29, 129,
   129–30
learning organizations   91–94
learning society   77–80
   market   86–88
   planning   83–84

reflexivity   84–86
   vision   80–83
lectures   58–59
lifelong learning   7, 66–69, 83,
   94–95
   and research   101
   universities and   107–08, 145
local regions   33–35, 106
   indigenous knowledge   45–46
   learning cities   88–91

management of universities
   99–100
markets   23
   corporate universities and
      116–17
   and learning society   86–88
   market place of learning   8–11
   see also learning industry
mega-universities   27, 72
mentoring   46, 71
meritocracy   23–24
modularization   121
moral role of universities   28–29
Motorola   113–14, 118, 120–22
multi-site universities   27, 138

nation states *see* state, the
National Technical University,
   USA   26
networks   26
NoonTime University   117

objective knowledge   42
Open University   15, 72, 86
operational competence   123
   see also practical knowledge
organizations, learning   91–94

part-time study   7
partnerships

with corporations 108–09
local 90–91
research 14–15, 51
patents 51, 52
PBL (problem-based learning) 70–71
political power 5
postgraduate education 7, 9, 101, 136, 136–37
power 23, 29, 91
practical knowledge 41, 46–47, *49*
learning 48–50
tacit knowledge 47–48
teaching 70–71
practice 15, 49
and theory 13, 70
practice placements 70
practitioner researchers 13, 75
pragmatism 12, 41, 42, 48–49, 126
Presenters University 117
problem-based learning (PBL) 70–71
process knowledge 46, 47, 48
publishing, book 59

quality 10, 118, 144

rationalism 11, 41
reason 41
reflexivity 84–86
regions *see* local regions
renewal, purposive 125
research 7, 50–53, 124, 137
changing nature 14–15
commercialization 51–52, 101–02
and learning 74–76
and lifelong learning 101
publication 59

research universities 14
residential education 16
risk society 84–85, 94

Scheler, Max 12–13, 42–43
schools 88–89
self-directed learning 139
self-scrutiny, collective 125
service role of universities 34–35, 89–91, 124
service sector 39, 40
social capital 33–34
social exclusion 24, 45, 79
social role of universities 7–8
society 77, 91
changes in 1–2, 4–5
and learning 68, 79
universities and 125–26
sponsorship of students 131
SRI International 133
Stanford University, USA 102
state, the 4, 6, 29–30
declining power 22, 23, 25
funding 8, 9, 14, 15
and universities 30–32
status of universities 3–6
students 6–8, 101
and corporate academies 106
learning 58–59
and moral issues 28–29
sponsorship 131
subjects, marketability 11
substructures 22, 25
superstructures 22, 25

tacit knowledge 47–48
teachers 17, *18*, 58
see also academic staff
teaching 27, 58, 60–61, 124
innovations in 69–71
see also learning

teaching universities   14
technology   21–22
theory and practice   13, 70
third age, universities of   69, 143,
   145
tolerance, communicative   126
training   67–68
   academic staff   103–04, 104–05
   local community   106
transnational corporations   22–23,
   29
transnational universities   27,
   138
truth   147–48
Tuomi, I   42

undergraduate education   6–7,
   135–36, 137
   continuing   100–01, 136
   funding   9
Universitas 21   26, 26–27
universities
   corporate academies   103–04,
      104–06
   corporate ethos and   96–97,
      97–102, 107–10
   and corporate universities   116
   corporate universities as
      122–28
   delivery of programmes   15–17
   discourse about   147–49
   and distance education   72–74
   distinctive features   145–47
   globalization opportunities
      25–27
   globalization problems   27–29
   and knowledge   11–13, 37, 44

knowledge dissemination
   58–60, 60, 61
knowledge management   55
   and learning industry   135–38,
      139
   and learning market   8–11, 87,
      88
   learning organizations   92, 95
   and learning society   82, 84, 85,
      87, 88
   and lifelong learning   69, 94,
      145
   and local regions   32–35, 46,
      88–91
   pressures and changes   1–3,
      18–19, 57
   and research   14–15, 51, 52–53,
      85
   state and   29–32
   status   3–6
   student clientele   6–8
   'university' concept   111,
      123–24, 124–26, 140–42,
      142–45, 149
University of Rapid Growth
   (UniRap)   122

validation procedures   10

Web, World Wide   16, 73–74, 134,
   138–39
welfare state   23, 31, 89
work, education and   30–31
work organization   98
work-based learning   71
World Bank knowledge
   management   54